Aesthetics and Design

Bloomsbury Aesthetics

Series Editor: Derek Matravers

The Bloomsbury Aesthetics series looks at the aesthetic questions and issues raised by all major art forms. Stimulating, engaging and accessible, the series offers food for thought not only for students of aesthetics, but also for anyone with an interest in philosophy and the arts.

Aesthetics and Film, by Katherine Thomson-Jones
Aesthetics and Literature, by David Davies
Aesthetics and Morality, by Elisabeth Schellekens Dammann
Aesthetics and Music, by Andy Hamilton
Aesthetics and Nature, by Glenn Parsons
Aesthetics and Nature (second edition), by Glenn Parsons
Aesthetics of Care, by Yuriko Saito
Architectural Aesthetics, by Edward Winters
Philosophy and Painting, by Jason Gaiger

Aesthetics and Design

The Value of Everyday Living

Jeffrey Petts

BLOOMSBURY ACADEMIC
LONDON • NEW YORK • OXFORD • NEW DELHI • SYDNEY

BLOOMSBURY ACADEMIC
Bloomsbury Publishing Plc
50 Bedford Square, London, WC1B 3DP, UK
1385 Broadway, New York, NY 10018, USA
29 Earlsfort Terrace, Dublin 2, Ireland

BLOOMSBURY, BLOOMSBURY ACADEMIC and the Diana logo are trademarks of Bloomsbury Publishing Plc

First published in Great Britain 2024

Cover design by Louise Dugdale
Cover image: 'The 1928 Dining Room', 1928. Artist: Charlotte Perriand.
Heritage Image Partnership Ltd / Alamy Stock Photo

A catalogue record for this book is available from the British Library.

ISBN: HB: 978-1-3502-1302-9
PB: 978-1-3502-1303-6
ePDF: 978-1-3502-1304-3
eBook: 978-1-3502-1305-0

Series: Bloomsbury Aesthetics

Typeset by RefineCatch Limited, Bungay, Suffolk
Printed and bound in Great Britain

To find out more about our authors and books visit www.bloomsbury.com and sign up for our newsletters.

Contents

Figures

Introduction

The problem of design

Aristotle reasoned – or perhaps was primarily *concerned* – that humankind must have a function otherwise its endeavours would be a 'pointless and ineffectual … infinite progression'.[1] Our work of designing and producing more things of increasingly dubious necessity seem only to confirm that concern. Indeed, without a proper understanding of human function and need, many things are produced for no good reason at all.

It is a scenario that concerns designers, and design critics and historians. Deyan Sudjic, director of the Design Museum in London from 2006 to 2020, suggests we live in 'a world drowning in objects'.[2] He points to homes packed with designed things. Sudjic raises the concern, echoing Aristotle's about proper human purpose, that most things are designed as mere consolations for our dull lives and that – before we throw them away – they 'infantilize us in our pursuit of them'.[3] If so, then design is essentially a function of consumerism, driven by purely commercial demands to sell things. Some designers, reflecting on the surfeit of things, admit 'we help companies shout at people from their TV, their phones, their streets. We don't care that nobody asked for it, that nobody needs it. We just want to sell, sell, sell, sell, sell.'[4] And: 'a lot of what we do is utterly useless. Tons of new products? Unnecessary'.[5] Even personal items of quality for personal use are perhaps only inspired by fashion and without a concern for function. Truly in that spirit, Andy Warhol commented, 'I don't wear a Tank watch to tell the time. In fact, I never wind it. I wear a Tank because it's the watch to wear.'[6] From Vogue's high-end 'Must-haves for the month' to IKEA's 'the wonderful everyday', most things seem designed primarily for status, fashion, and lifestyle, to the extent they might almost all seem gratuitous.

Sudjic's concerns reflect those of many in the design profession to the extent that by 2021 the Design Museum in London hosted an exhibition called 'Waste Age', suggesting there is an endemic 'problem of design'. In short, that design work is so entwined with consumerism, with 'too much stuff', that 'waste is not merely culture's by-product but that it *is* culture – and that we have produced a culture of waste'.[7] The existence of a vast marine gyre of debris from plastic designed products, the 'Great Pacific garbage patch', is evidence of the adverse environmental consequences: evidence and symbolic of our Waste Age. The UK's Design Council's mission statement thus focuses on environmental concerns linked to over-production. It acknowledges that 'design shapes the world and we need to re-design nearly every aspect of how we live our lives to tackle the climate emergency'.[8] So, it continues: 'we need to accelerate the process of making design part of the solution. Designers, business, government and communities need to design in a way that is regenerative and make the planet a key stakeholder in everything they do.'[9] Yet here too, then, is the positive idea that design can *solve* problems: it can shape the world for good not just toward 'waste' (of materials, lives, and the environment).

Design got to this situation via the optimism of mid-twentieth-century American consumerism. But, even at its apogee, the idea of a utopian 'Cornucopia City' – ever-expanding sales and no personal, social, or environmental side-effects – was challenged, and its proponents, businesses and the designers constantly designing new products for them, were described as 'waste makers'. Vance Packard pictured a coming future where 'the heart of Cornucopia City will be occupied by a titanic push-button super mart built to simulate a fairyland'.[10] He mockingly suggested that then we will shop to our heart's content with 'no jangling cash registers to disrupt the holiday mood'.[11] Packard identified three different ways in which products can be made obsolescent, so that endless shopping can be maintained, calling them the obsolescence of function, of quality, and of desirability.[12] While the first is noted as laudable when planned, Packard's analysis focused on marketing strategies that deliberately created obsolescence via quality and desirability. Still, designers designed the 'new' products. For Packard, these products were not only wasteful but wasted our lives.

A parallel criticism of the role of design in creating waste and poorer experiential lives was made in the 1950s by the architectural critic Ian Nairn when he warned of 'Subtopia' in the built environment. He described it as a 'world of universal low-density mess', a world 'made with human artefacts, often inoffensive in themselves, disastrous in the places, quantities and associations in which they are found'.[13] In this world, planners and designers are the prime 'agents' of Subtopia and the world of useless ugly things.[14]

The idea that our lives are somehow wasted, experientially less than they might be through over-consumption, and that design is complicit is echoed now by the designer Kenya Hara's observations of Japan's consumer culture (and it applies to all consumer cultures). He notes how it has changed how we feel about the things we buy and use and about what constitutes happiness. He believes that 'we've unconsciously become overly tolerant of a Japan overflowing with things'; we've become insensitive to the abnormality of over-buying.[15] Indeed, something has 'confounded the scale by which we sense happiness'.[16] Still, Hara sees the answer to this situation in design. Designers, through the quality of their products, must re-educate consumers about what is truly desirable. Hara calls this, overall, designing a culture built on aesthetics.

Is this merely design marching to a different commercial tune? Or is something fundamental at stake about restoring the true nature of design? The 'Waste Age' exhibition notes that designers mass producing good-quality products for all at affordable prices was an active and laudable aim of design, even if misappropriated by the drive for ever-increasing sales and economic growth.[17] And so, we see in fact that the 'problem of design', that design only produces 'too much of low quality', is a familiar theme in the history of design work. But it is one that, significantly from an aesthetic and philosophical perspective, draws attention to the essence of design proper or good design: that is, that it necessarily involves qualitative factors related both to products and our everyday lives with them.

So, in the 1930s, for example, Lord Sempill, then chairman of the UK's Design and Industries Association, observed that 'we now have far more possessions than our grandfathers . . . [but we are] discovering that quantity is not enough to make a real civilization; quality is of equal importance'.[18] He also noted that the English designer William Morris was 'the first to preach this' some fifty years earlier.[19] In the meantime, however, he noted that 'millions of senseless ugly objects' continued to be made and that 'vast new towns' were growing 'without plan or beauty'.[20] Morris is regarded as a pioneer of modern design and so his realization of the problem of design at its outset supports the idea that questions of quality and over-production and their aesthetic, experiential effects is central to thinking about design work.

Still, in the spirit of Morris, a recent general introduction to design, for example, describes design's 'shared interest in improving society'; its necessarily 'optimistic and forward-looking' approach; and its aspiration to make humans stronger, more adept, and able to manage their environment.[21] For Dieter Rams, in a similar vein, these translate to key design principles about 'innovation' and 'usefulness' (as well as 'aesthetics').[22] So, he argues that technology offers opportunities to innovate with original designs. Additionally, products are useful by what he calls 'psychological' as well as strictly functional criteria, given that they are 'used every day and have an effect on people and their well-being'.[23] Design awards, like the UK's Design Museum Designs of the Year, also routinely refer to similar overarching aims around designs that promote 'new ways of living' and 'user experience that will improve lives'.[24]

In 2019, Sudjic replayed design's dilemma: its commendable aims to improve everyday lives and yet its seeming production only of 'waste'. He notes that design's 'idea of activism', the pursuit of a civilized world of beautiful things, has been 'swept aside by militant consumerism' in the 1980s.[25] But he also noted 'the rediscovery of those activist ideas by a new generation, one that believes the purpose of design is to change the world, rather than to function as a kind of marketing'.[26] By 2020, the Covid pandemic and ever-increasing evidence of climate change had brought such activist ideas into focus as designers thought about their role in remaking the world.[27] Remaking it, indeed, to be 'a healthier, kinder and more equal world'.[28] Recognition of the environmental consequences of economic growth, of the surfeit of things, has only heightened attention to what we make.[29] Fundamental, existential, thinking about 'what design is' is evident too in, for example, these questions posed to contemporary designers. 'What is the right pace? ... How can we set a system to consistently create great work, week after week? Should we even expect ourselves to be capable of that? ... Do we run too fast to check if we are running in the right direction? ... Will we manage to find the right pace? [ending with the plea, almost] What does it even mean?'[30]

Why is the problem of design an issue for philosophical aesthetics? Can philosophical inquiry help deal with the evident angst of designers about their role in our wasteful lives? The problem of design clearly invokes questions about what humans need to live well and about what constitutes quality in design. The 'problem of design' – construed as the best mass production of things of everyday use and designing our shared built environment – is a philosophical problem because it is fundamentally one about important, disputable concepts

– namely, function, need, and flourishing. And it is a problem in philosophical aesthetics because these concepts necessarily engage thinking about the nature of aesthetic interest, experience, and value.

A metacritical approach

A metacritical approach to design takes what designers say about good design in general seriously and aims to understand what they *mean* by the terms they typically use.[31] Their critical thinking about their work, about designing, *per se*, is about the general value of design work. So, while it refers to the range of evaluative criteria used in assessing individual designs, it also expresses general 'apologies' for design. These statements about design work form the most significant material for metacriticism, establishing both the general value ascribed to design as an activity and, significantly, feeding back into specific evaluations of designs. I argue for aesthetic functionalism about design based on analyses of these issues as initially stated by designers.

Part I's three chapters set design in its philosophical contexts. Chapter 1 presents the landscape of thinking philosophically about design. I map broad areas covered by 'Design Studies' (which draws on sociology, anthropology, as well as philosophy, and from many traditions and areas in examining design practices and thinking) and the philosophy of design, although I do pay special attention to the work of Albert Borgmann, Glenn Parsons, and Jane Forsey. I note problems associated with the absence of any agreed key concepts or theoretic approaches; as well as a notable absence of enquiry into what designers say about design in general. But I also present the best philosophical lines of enquiry for design from within these areas. There are other notable contributions to thinking philosophically about design which do not map neatly to Design Studies or the philosophy of design: in particular, I focus on thoughts on the true nature of design work by David Pye, and Roger Scruton after Ludwig Wittgenstein.

In Chapter 2, I note that all designers with a general interest in design work beyond their specialist area of design have stated, one way or another, in essays or interviews or manifestos, why they think design is important to the purpose and quality of human life. A metacritical approach based on philosophical analysis of these general statements by designers about the aims and value of their work establishes a general 'design apology'. I examine a range of designers' statements about the nature and aims of their work, including Charlotte Perriand and Dieter Rams. Apologies answer questions like 'what makes design a good thing to have in one's life?' Designers couch their work in the prosaic terminology of 'need', 'function', and 'problem-solving'. But I shall argue that their 'apologies' for design are conceived in terms of 'improvement', 'fit', 'well-being', and related terms. Furthermore, they are properly understood within an account of aesthetic experience as an adaptive and consummatory experience. In short, when designers talk about the general value of design, they do so on the grounds that it delivers that kind of experience. Designers' apologies for design then are essentially aesthetic defences of design; the composite 'design apology' is an aesthetic account of the value of design in our everyday lives and supports aesthetic functionalism about design. Aesthetic functionalism about design amounts to a cluster of criteria around meeting user needs in fitting ways that improve everyday life, adding things of beauty, of aesthetic value, to everyday lives, and creating built environments and communities that aid the good life. From the design apology, we can adduce that design work has several key components of, I will argue, connected philosophical, conceptual interest, namely need, function, flourishing, aesthetic experience, and value. I examine the design apology in the light of philosophical analyses of these core concepts.

While Chapter 2 places design in the context of everyday aesthetics, this area of study is supposed new to philosophical aesthetics, and in Chapter 3 I examine this movement, and how its issues relate to design's. So, I address some general philosophical issues in everyday aesthetics in the light of aesthetic functionalism about design. I argue that design is properly a core concern of the aesthetics of the everyday, both as subject matter and in contributing resolutions to its fundamental debates, especially about the nature and value of everyday aesthetic experience. I also examine the idea of 'world-making' in the Everyday Aesthetics movement, as developed by Yuriko Saito in *Aesthetics of the Familiar*, and ideas of aesthetic education more generally, including the 'education of desire' suggested by Kenya Hara, in the context of design's aims and work.

Concluding Part I with thoughts on design's role in aesthetic education and world-making at large, I turn in Part II to actual design work and how the design apology plays out in design's three main areas. So, Part II's three chapters focus on those different areas of design work: broadly, products, homes, and cities.

Chapter 4 focuses on design as an activity concerned with mass-produced useful objects made to serve a specific purpose. I argue that good designs meet both functional and aesthetic conditions. These two criteria are thematic in product design. But their character and relationship are less clearcut. So, I examine ideas of need, beauty, and style; but also, their necessary relations to the need for products and so to problem-solving. In examining product designers' views on their work – including Charles and Ray Eames, Raymond Loewy, and contemporary designers – and examples of how needs and products change though examples from the history and practice of design, the richness and complexity of the functionality and aesthetic experience of everyday things emerges, challenging engineering or austerely functional views of good design work.

Design also has a concern with that band of aesthetic interest at the everyday, household level that lies between the design and appreciation of individual products and that of the built environment: I examine that in Chapter 5. The idea of improving one's home life through product choices informs high-end design and fashion magazines like *World of Interiors*, *Vogue*, *Dwell*, and *Cabana* as well as IKEA's marketing. Still, designers continue to express a larger claim about the purpose of their work designing our everyday domestic lives. I trace a history of this idea in the work of Christopher Dresser and the development of product ranges and specialist stores, for example, and its links to late nineteenth-century Aestheticism and ideas about artistic taste in the home. I also connect it to Scandinavian design principles and ideas about the societal role of a properly designed domestic life. It all amounts to another expression of the design apology, namely that good design in our everyday, domestic surroundings goes beyond momentary and fashionable lifestyle choices, dependent on our incomes, to creating the conditions necessary for everyday aesthetic lives. But can home life be designed? Should it be? These questions challenge how designers use notions of need, function, and aesthetic experience in contexts beyond the efficacy of individual products. Questions of a social and political character arise when designing home life is examined, prefiguring overtly utopian design schemes for whole communities, including mass housing.

I turn to those issues in Chapter 6. Examples like garden cities, Werkbund estates in Germany, the UK's New Towns, Chandigarh in India, American and British public housing, have indicated the design apology's various utopian aspirations. I connect design's utopian aims to utopian thinking more generally, separating truly aesthetic and functional ideals from political ones in the process. I focus analysis too on the failures of mass housing projects to meet design aims in the twentieth century. Utopian aspirations persist though, given renewed impetus by environmental issues of sustainability and the design solutions offered by so-called smart cities. The idea that urban areas can, in the process, also be designed for happiness and aesthetic experience is also examined. Aesthetic understanding of need, function, and flourishing is, again, central to the analysis of design's work and aims, and to what aesthetic effects the good design of cities can realistically achieve.

Still, what good design provides experientially is unique and exceptional, and the Conclusion explores its possibilities as well as limits.

Part One

Design and philosophy

1

Design from philosophical perspectives

Introduction

This chapter sets out the *topography* of existing philosophically minded accounts of design. I say minded because much of the area can only be described as philosophical in the everyday meaning of the word as generally reflective or questioning. A multi-disciplinary approach has coalesced into 'Design Studies' or 'Design Philosophy', drawing on sociology, anthropology, as well as philosophy, and from many theoretic traditions within them. Rather than map all these, I take Albert Borgmann's important essay on the 'depth of design' as a good guide to areas of philosophical concern addressed by design studies in general. I also give due attention to the avowedly philosophical and aesthetic analyses of design by Glenn Parsons and Jane Forsey. There are other notable contributions to thinking philosophically about design which do not map neatly to Design Studies or the philosophy of design: in particular, I focus on thoughts on the true nature of design work by David Pye, Ludwig Wittgenstein, and Roger Scruton.

A common problem for proper philosophical inquiry into design work is illustrated, I believe, by this overview. That is the absence of detailed analyses of the statements designers make about the nature of design work, over and above their reflections on their own practical work. From that observation, it becomes clearer too that fundamental concepts of wide philosophical significance and interest driving design work are either neglected in design studies and existing philosophy of design, like the concept of need and associated ideas of human flourishing, or misunderstood, like the concepts of function and everyday aesthetic experience and value. This chapter, then, is also a general prompt for a different, metacritical approach to ground and structure the philosophical aesthetics of design.

Design studies

In 2000, reviewing a selection of six books on design from the 1990s, Janet McCracken noted both good and bad things about how design was treated philosophically.[1] The 'bad' included a tendency to 'empty academic polemicizing'.[2] She added that the overall philosophical value of books in design studies is 'hard to figure' and their logic can be 'rambling and obscure'.[3] However, some 'good' was also noted, especially where design studies engaged 'methodologies of design education' and the role of designed commodities in 'the good life'.[4]

McCracken's general observations of Design Studies reflect its variety of theoretical approaches, source material, and aims. So, approaches range across analytical and continental philosophy but also include the social sciences and cultural studies. Within broadly philosophical approaches alone, there are different emphases on the roles of aesthetics, ethics, and economic and political philosophy. And fundamentally, what *is* the subject matter? Is it designed things, consumer products? Or the statements of designers on the nature of their work? Both, in relation to each other? And does it properly go beyond the concerns of contemporary design in specialist areas like graphics, kitchenware, homes, and so on, to general issues about how we should live with products and built places?

Design Studies was prefigured by quasi-academic journals like the *Everyday Art Quarterly* (1946–53), which changed its title to the *Design Quarterly* and ran until 1996. This at least focused thoughtful commentary on designers and modern designs of everyday products. Now, an academic journal dedicated to design, *Design Issues*, has design history, theory, and criticism as its subject; and its approach is unspecified other than to provoke inquiry into design's cultural and intellectual issues. These two types of study of design have morphed too into specialist design journals and magazines for specialisms like graphic design or home interiors, often combining advertising and lifestyle pieces with reflective essays by academics.

So, little if anything has changed since McCracken's overview of the subject. From 2016, *The Routledge Companion to Design Studies* presents an eclectic and wide-ranging set of interests and approaches: but they are described as 'sharply focused, nuanced, and clever speculations'.[5] So, from design's mid-twentieth-century focus on modern products, a reviewer observes an area of study that 'has spiraled out to encompass a breathtaking array of domains, and so I began to notice the absence of work on design as it is and has been consumed'.[6] I ask, similarly, is Design Studies addressing its actual subject matter, the experience and value of everyday objects of use, of designed things, places, and communities? Issues around sustainable design, the good life, and design activism, to give some important examples, arise from everyday design work. But what is it about design work that makes that so? Without that understanding, disputable notions of sustainability, aesthetic and ethical living, and political aims, might falsely *direct* design work.

If the vast terrain of disciplines and approaches associated with design make a detailed survey impossible, still it is possible and useful to identify design studies that do engage the basic concerns of design work and should be the basis of philosophical inquiry. So, McCracken notes Albert Borgmann's contribution to *Discovering Design: Explorations in Design Studies*, and his contention 'that designers as the guardians of common practical wisdom ... [help] people engage more meaningfully with their daily environment'.[7] He recognizes that design practice is properly the subject of philosophical investigation and asks questions like 'is design an art or a science?' and 'what knowledge does it require?'

Borgmann's same essay on design features in a later anthology on 'design philosophy', perhaps because his analysis retains its value in highlighting key concepts and subjects for the philosophical aesthetics of design. He recognizes that thinking about design philosophically starts with the ideas of 'function' and 'quality'. Borgmann contends that design amounts to more than 'safety, efficiency and commodiousness'.[8] While I will argue later that these are qualitative aspects of a functioning design, Borgmann connects qualitative aspects of design to its larger concern with 'the excellence of material culture' as a whole.[9] By this he means it shapes our everyday lives in profound ways. Designers, then, are properly vocationally charged with a responsibility: with 'this precious social good' that sits alongside matters of 'health, justice, and education'. In short, designers 'are charged with making the material culture conducive to engagement'.[10]

For Borgmann, the qualitative aspect of design is that it must be 'engaging'. It must counter the idea that excellence resides in 'attenuation, superficiality, and even disappearance'.[11] He gives examples, like developments in sound reproduction. Borgmann, writing in the 1990s, anticipated a world when 'a hand-held device consisting of a small keyboard and screen ... allows you to call up whatever and however much music you desire'. The result will be that 'the designer's scope will be reduced to making ... surfaces as pleasing and the programming device as portable and functional as possible'. Why is this presented as problematic? Borgmann sees in it a move from aesthetic design to engineering design. Moreover, it reflects a shift from user engagement to user 'disburdenment'.[12] Now, of course, music can be requested as basically as a voice-activated request for a device to 'play me some pop music'. It extends, no doubt, to our whole 'just-one-click' culture of buying and using things. Still, what is practically and philosophically alarming about such design? Isn't 'ease of use', removing 'burdens' from everyday living, a fundamental design principle?

Borgmann appeals to the idea that our fullest and most rewarding interactions with designed things requires designed things that engage far more than our ability to state what we want, to press a button, and get it. Rather, 'the most commanding and subtle things engage our talents most fully; and ... to employ our capacities most deeply we turn to the most powerful and intricate things'.[13] For example, 'a musical instrument normally engages a person deeply; a television program typically fails to do so'.[14] And contrast the engagement with a cooking pot's 'shape, weight, heat conductivity, surface texture, even the sound it makes when you stir in it' to using a microwave.[15] Borgmann appeals to the pleasures of cooking with well-designed products. It is the kind of description that often provides the marketing for products: I think of my Sori Yanagi kettle and its accompanying blurb about how Yanagi 'designed many works which enriched daily life'. Borgmann provides examples meant to illustrate that good designs evidence good engineering for experiential goals: for aesthetic experiences of 'walking, sitting, reading, eating, conversing, shopping, and playing'.[16] Aesthetic design has become shallow, for Borgmann, because it is limited to the surface appearance of things. So, 'aesthetic design becomes shallow, not because it is aesthetic, but because it has become superficial'.[17]

It is important to note, then, that Borgmann is appealing to a notion of aesthetic experience beyond some appreciation of the form of things. And beyond our pleasure in consumption. Disburdened from any exertion or exercise of skill by engineering design – with aesthetic design restricted to styling and smooth interfaces – our engagement with designs is correspondingly restricted to the enjoyments of consuming 'opaque and glamorous commodities'.[18] Borgmann's ultimate appeal is to a notion of aesthetic experience that is beyond the visual. And to the idea that, with that in mind, good design works with the tactile and motile in our engagement with things.

I have focused on Borgmann's account because its description of the 'depth of design' relies on several key concepts in philosophical aesthetics that provide the basis of my analysis. I believe – and will argue the case – that he is correct about design's essential aesthetic character, about how this is related to ways of engaging with designs. This experiential concern deepens design's work beyond the purely functional, engineering requirements of everyday products of use. In short, then, design is central to our aesthetic lives. Similarly, McCracken concluded her overview of design studies by noting how Borgmann rightly makes a case for design as a key feature of humanistic thought and that there is much at stake when it is considered beyond engineering and styling and as a social activity. I concur that Borgmann helps challenge any scepticism about the philosophical significance of 'vacuum cleaners, cars, typographical fonts, or teapots'.[19] But Borgmann's examples are disputable. Our engagement with reproduced music, for example, does not require prolonged and skilful engagement with the sound system; designs that minimalize that and enhance listening to our choice of music are not disengaging us from aesthetic experiences. Intuitively too, we think that some needs *should* be met with ease and require the minimum of skill and exertion. Borgmann's examples – while still revealing the personal and cultural significance of the experience of designed things – reveal the philosophical requirement to attend more closely to the concept of need and aesthetic experience and value. So, to fulfil the challenge of arguing the 'depth of design' requires fuller philosophical investigation of design's core concepts – namely, need, function, aesthetic experience, and quality.[20]

Philosophy of design

Introducing *The Design Philosophy Reader*, its editor conceded that while the pervasiveness of design should make it a 'major topic of investigation', it is 'rarely engaged by philosophers'.[21] More than a 'design is everywhere' claim for philosophical interest, Borgmann's account of its personal and social value and significance should properly be the motivation and structure for a philosophy of design. And that value and significance stems ultimately from its concern, above all, with human needs.

Yet, Willis's editorial introduction to 'design philosophy' is sceptical that design work's thinking is properly concerned with real needs: any 'philosophical' thought from designers is just the profession reflecting on its processes for the purpose of practical instruction for designers. Willis characterizes it as the everyday working of a 'service profession', where the ultimate service is to capitalism, to designing things that will sell, and to making profits for designers' clients.[22] Against that backdrop, Willis contends that 'Design Philosophy' is, instead, 'what design could be, what it needs to be, and to become'.[23] The collection is characterized as 'hybrid, trans, or even post-disciplinary and dominantly oriented toward a politicized reading of design'.[24] It is not 'philosophy *of* design', then, but a curated selection of philosophical writings that support a particular view of what design should be. With this approach to the subject, there is no reference that aesthetics is the branch of philosophical inquiry best suited to examine design's fundamental principles and practices.

So, the problem of identifying any philosophical analysis of design's key concepts remains. A work like *Design: Key Concepts* by D. J. Huppatz seems obviously promising especially in asking 'what is design?'[25] But it is soon evident that the aim of the book, however laudable, is not met by philosophical inquiry into key design concepts. Huppatz wants to define 'design' because it is 'little understood outside professional circles, yet vitally important across a range of fields'.[26] The aim is to present a framework that holds together disparate theorizing about design from multiple sources. So, 'design' is described as a 'fluid term' used by 'design professionals – communication, industrial interior and interaction designers, as well as architects and engineers', who, it is stated, all use the term in different ways.[27] Huppatz adds artists, scientists, and politicians into the mix of those interested in design. But Huppatz's definition is immediately problematic: design is said to be about conceiving a plan of action for a particular outcome, with the only proviso being that such plans must aim to improve the human experience. This is not a definition of design work since it clearly applies to planning many things, as singular and undesigned as birthday parties for example, that are not about mass producing things of everyday use. Huppatz does provide many examples of design work. But there is no conceptual analysis of design. Rather, general themes related to examples of design work are stated, like 'interaction, emotion, sustainability, accessibility and participation'.[28]

Failures, like Huppatz's, to address the fundamental concerns of design might, perhaps, be addressed by appealing to pre-philosophic, common and garden, intuitions about design work that still resonate within the broad community of designers, marking a supposed basic fault line in design practice between 'engineering' and 'styling'.[29] One intuition is broadly functional. It understands design work as essentially making things that fulfil their basic function, requiring the appropriate problem-solving and engineering or technical skills for that type of thing. A second intuition is broadly aesthetic. It understands design work as essentially a discrete activity concerned with giving functional things a stylish 'look and feel' or form and requiring broadly creative and artistic skills. In other words, the functionalist intuition sees design as solving problems about how something will work, and its exemplary worker is an engineer-designer. In contrast, the aestheticist intuition sets any design problem as one about a functional thing's form and supposed aesthetic appeal, and designers are essentially 'creatives'. How far does this basic division take us in the proper philosophical analysis of design?

Two recent dedicated, philosophical analyses of design are by Glenn Parsons and Jane Forsey. Their radically different approaches and conclusions about design suggest philosophical understanding of basic intuitions and concepts associated with function and the aesthetic is far from resolved.

Glenn Parsons makes a 'sketch of the terrain of a philosophy of design', aiming to 'bring together existing philosophical work in a systematic treatment'; he adds that it is 'a philosophical approach to a hitherto unexplored topic'.[30] The latter claim is evidently false since design work has been subject to theoretic exploration – questions about its guiding principles and true purpose, for example – since its inception. I offer this range of philosophically minded thinkers about design, for example: William Morris, William Lethaby, Walter Gropius, Le Corbusier, Charlotte Perriand, Anthony Bertram, Herbert Read, John Dewey, Ludwig Wittgenstein, David Pye, Roger Scruton, Dieter Rams, Kenya Hara, Dejan Sudjic, etc.[31]

That aside for now, Parsons adopts a strategy of 'using a Modernist template' and reconstructing 'key Modernist ideas'.[32] Again though, this immediately throws reasonable doubt on the comprehensiveness of the analysis being presented. That is for one simple reason: designers do not work only to modernist templates and ideas. That is evident in the range of products we all see for sale.

Still, perhaps, philosophic analysis reveals a hidden universal modernism running through design work and products? So, what about Parsons's definition of design, does that support the idea? Parsons defines design as 'the intentional solution of a problem, by the creation of plans for a new sort of thing, where the plans would not be immediately seen, by a reasonable person, as an inadequate solution'.[33] The definition therefore contains 'intentionality', 'creativity', and 'adequacy' conditions. The 'intentionality' condition is a given since design necessarily involves plans for functional things. Parsons's 'creativity' and 'adequacy' conditions are also necessary within what we would ordinarily understand as design work; but their descriptions in terms of 'newness', as plans for new sorts of things, and 'reasonable judgement' are questionable. A reasonable description of design work starts with its conception of a design problem, from recognizing a product's core or descriptively functional aspects (what a product must do to be a product of its type) to its normatively functional possibilities (to deliver putative social and environmental goals, for example). It seems right to say then that product design depends on designers being cognisant of the functional requirements that a project to make something sets. To amplify a little, it includes the core or simple function(s) of a product (scissors that cut, for example), but also specific or complex functions that meet particular needs (cutting cloth and being safe to use), and cultural or normative functions (made of wholly recyclable materials, to complete the example). Tall office buildings and housing estates present different functional requirements and so generate different kinds of design problems. Different design problems create the conditions for different design solutions, for different, and in that sense new, products. Within that broad description of design work, a design, then, would be necessarily 'new' only in so far as a designer understands a design problem confronts a unique set of circumstances. Design's 'newness' has a particular meaning then, referring properly to creativity in conceiving design problems and solutions for functional things. Parsons does acknowledge that the design process includes conceiving design problems with function and client restraints, safety, branding style, legal requirements, and so on all included. But he disregards how this description of design must qualify the 'creativity' condition of design from his 'creating a new sort of thing' to 'rethinking a design problem and solution' for making a functional thing. So, rethinking a design would also seem to have less to do with Parsons's notion of 'reasonable judgement' supporting the adequacy of a design, and be rather a matter of imagination and 'trial and error' testing of a product, of iterative practical judgement.

Parsons places modernism's 'humanist approach to good design' as central to its contribution to the philosophy of design.[34] Its humanism is a result of its functionalism about design. Whether this insight and contribution is unique to modernism is disputable. Not least because designers routinely work to design things of everyday use. Functionalism about design offers, at least, philosophic insight into understanding a central feature of its work, namely the proper conception of design problems: that is, taking full account of both basic functional requirements and the norms and cultural aspirations associated with the products in question. Modernism may well, in its theoretic focus on function, be *illustrative* of this general philosophic insight. But Parsons's stronger claim for modernism is doubtful, namely that its stylistic eschewal of ornamentation (after Adolf Loos) further exemplifies (along with its functionalism) the humanist approach and proper general understanding of design. So, consider Parsons's claim that, for example, chairs can never have 'expressive power or meaning'.[35] Florence de Dampierre's history of chairs argues that sitting has been something of a luxurious human activity and that things to sit on were invented for status and comfort, evidence of civilized behaviour.[36] Parsons only sees this as symbolism, as expressive of zeitgeist, never as internal to a design problem's proper conception and as varied and open as our interpretations of, for example, 'civilized' for the object being made. Similar problems relate to Parsons's defence of modernism's account of 'form and function'. In arguing that modernism 'curtails expression in design and puts function to the fore' Parsons risks confusing modernist style for a genuine philosophic insight about design work in general.[37] In fact, curtailing considerations of 'expression' in conceiving a design problem is a choice unwarranted by any philosophic considerations (though it will be important for a modernist designer conceiving a design problem in modernist terms).

Parsons's modernist line on the whole philosophy of design leads him to exclude aesthetic considerations from any defining role in design work. His claim for the independence of aesthetic considerations, that they lie outside a design problem's conception, is passed to Jerrold Levinson to support in terms of his account of aesthetic properties. So, Levinson's 'approach [aesthetic realism] fits nicely with design, where we tend to take in the aesthetics of things in a transient way, as we are busily engaged with our everyday activities'.[38] But Levinson's aesthetic realism, where aesthetic properties are distinct from their structural bases, is surely arguable in the case of designed functional products, where use of a product is properly considered as an integrated experience of 'functioning well'. But that, I concede, depends on understanding the aesthetics of design in terms of experience of a product's form in use; moreover that 'aesthetic' refers to something more than the trivial, pleasing appearance of a thing, and more strongly to notions and experiences of 'fit'. I return to these issues in the section entitled 'The nature of design' when noting thinkers about design work, like David Pye and Ludwig Wittgenstein, who have seen it in fundamentally aesthetic terms.

Finally, there is a third set of issues with Parsons's scoping and analysis of the philosophy of design, namely his view of design's 'ethics'. While it is evidently true and welcome for a complete philosophical aesthetics of design to see theorized that 'design is important because it creates the material and virtual environment', the whole basis of this importance lies, surely, in the lives that are engendered in making and using well-designed products, and these grounds are hardly explored by Parsons.[39] Rather, Parsons looks to external factors to explain how design can meet existing ethical obligations, ignoring the factors internal to good design work – in essence the requirement to properly conceive a design problem with human needs in mind – which entail ethical products. Of course, in passing, a designer faced with a brief to design a product that will kill faces an overriding moral decision: it is not a moral constituent of a design problem like others which can be built into a design problem's conception, like social and environmental concerns. In other words, Parsons is right to introduce the ethical dimension in any broad consideration of design. But his conclusion that it is a dimension beyond designers' work (he speculates that philosophers should do it, working with designers) again misconstrues the openness and essential normativity (inclusive of ethical considerations, even of modernism's utopianism) of the 'design problem' as a philosophic concept. So, Parsons's claims to scoping, sourcing, and structuring the philosophy of design is exaggerated, even as a 'sketch' of the field. The text is, perhaps, better regarded as a piece on the contribution of architectural modernism to the broader aim of a whole philosophy of design. Understanding modernism's contribution needs to take account of its avowedly revolutionary ambitions for architecture in the twentieth century, succinctly expressed as: 'After WWII, architecture was going to save the world.'[40] Architectural modernism was intimately connected to ideas about the effectiveness of science and engineering to solve social problems, especially related to mass housing and improving the kinds of everyday, practical lives led in them. Societies would be made better places to live. Such an understanding of modernism as a political movement should limit, or at the very least caution against, any ambition to build a whole philosophy of design on its foundations.[41]

In summary: Parsons's definition of design is seriously flawed by relying exclusively on modernism to supply both examples of design work and theoretic support. Modernism is pre- and post-dated by other non-industrial and non-Western design practices and accounts (everything from late Neolithic Chinese work to wabi-sabi and post-factory digital making). More significantly, modernism does not supply all there is that designers say and do. Modernism's contribution to the philosophy of design is significant; but that is largely in drawing attention to, rather than examining and resolving, the centrality of function and its relations to the aesthetic. Finally, Parsons's modernist understanding of design work undermines his account of its ethical value, since it fails to understand the kind of everyday design problems designers solve and the appeals to user experiences of their products that involves. Still, Parsons does cover a range of issues essential for any comprehensive philosophy of design, for all its flaws related to adequately describing, and thus understanding, actual design work.

In Jane Forsey's *Aesthetics of Design*, there is similar proposed attention to design work, to the relations between function and the aesthetic, and to design's supposed ethical role. Forsey does acknowledge the everyday aesthetic significance of design but without sufficient attention on designers and the nature of their work; and of critical appraisals of designs. It is rather, an account of the concept of beauty, exclusively Kantian, and how it applies to designed things like pens and coffee pots as well as paintings and well-made craft objects. Forsey states that 'the Kantian notion of dependent beauty, as a unique form of judgement, provides the most cogent model for understanding design excellence. And it is with this notion that we can best understand our particular aesthetic experiences of design.'[42] Dependent beauty is a kind of beauty 'that does presuppose . . . a concept [of what the object ought to be] and the perfection of the object in accordance therewith.'[43] With that in mind, Forsey concludes a lengthy discussion of Kantian beauty with the example of 'two coffee pots, mine and his.'[44] 'His' always looks new and shiny; 'hers' has become dull, rotted and a little rusty. But Forsey claims that a Kantian account of dependent beauty explains why she is correct to judge her coffee pot beautiful and his less than it seems. It comes down to the simple fact that his pot burns your fingers on use. Hers does not; it is easier to clean too. These are indeed features that concern designers and attract our attention as users. But Forsey leaves us with what I will call the 'coffee pot dilemma' for philosophical aesthetics, revealing its requirement still to examine design in the light of design's core concepts of need, function, and experience and value.

Designed things are designed to work well. They are user tested and mass produced to that end. We judge things working well in our use of them. That experience is not divided by considerations of free (looks good) and dependent (works well) beauty. That bifurcated experience does not apply to designs *qua* designs. It is not a part of good design work to design things that do not function well.[45] Designers aim at integrated experiences of things 'working well'. So, there is no experiential beauty in a coffee pot that burns one's fingers and is hard to clean. To think it might still be 'freely' beautiful because of its 'sleek conical shape and shiny brass handle' is simply outside the scope of design work and therefore of any aesthetics *of design*.[46]

Forsey's contribution is important though because it does set design in the context of function and experience. And because she identifies our aesthetic experiences in using designed things. But it fails in terms of the theoretic setting of dependent beauty. The experiential richness of engaging with designed things – something noted in Borgmann and in design studies more generally – and the importance of that to personal and social development is ignored in Forsey or treated as an unhelpful incursion of moral requirements for good design.[47] Again, this adds support to the suggestion that the concept of need, especially associated with flourishing, helps bridge the gap between the functional and the aesthetic when thinking about design.

We get a little nearer to setting design within ideas of everyday needs and aesthetic experiences in the analyses of the essential nature of design by David Pye and Roger Scruton, which includes a 'bit of help from Wittgenstein'.[48]

The nature of design

David Pye's *Nature of Design* is profoundly sceptical about the paradigmatic account of design in terms of 'function', claiming that function is never sufficiently clear or pure such that form follows function, the famous dictum of architectural modernism and scientific functionalism more generally, coined by Louis Sullivan at the turn of the twentieth century. Nor do things ever really work: of designed things 'we can always say what it ought to do, but that it never does'.[49] Rather,

> in useful design and making there has from the first been a steady insistence on the doing of useless work. We might perhaps expect that early stone implements at least would have been strictly utilitarian, but it was not so. Even some palaeolithic tools are considered to have been made with better workmanship than was needed to make them get results.[50]

He terms this additional supposedly non-functional work that designers necessarily do as 'useless work'.[51] Pye concludes that '"function" ... is a wonderful hindrance to any understanding of design and will die hard, for it makes a fairly intricate subject look simple'.[52]

The account is puzzling not least because some designed things simply do work while others do not. From the palaeolithic use of stone tools to the present, there is evidence of that. What changes over time are the functional requirements of, for example, cutting. Also, Pye's idea of 'useless work' seems paradoxical when used to describe 'good workmanship'. What criteria of 'good' is being used? Theoretically, Pye does not provide an answer and deliberately so. Pye's notion of 'useless work' is best understood as a rhetorical device. It is used by him to indicate that 'function' conceived as purely utilitarian is a fiction. Rather, 'function' proper is 'fairly intricate'.[53] Also, what is thought falsely 'functional' is in fact anything that is designed and 'made as economically as possible with their [products] being efficient'.[54] So-called 'useless work' is in fact, as I understand Pye's rhetorical stance against engineering design, the good work that designers do if they attend to all the complexities of any design problem they are charged to solve. And that is more than 'economizing'. When Pye equates 'function' with conceiving a design problem in terms simply of 'cheapness' and a 'minimal look', as he does, then he uses the term in a pejorative or deflationary sense to make a point about the potential richness of designed things (and that they'll ultimately 'not really work' in so far as there is no ultimate, engineered endgame of designed things). Understood otherwise, he is plainly wrong about design work, which clearly is deeply concerned with designing things that function and that work well, here and now.

Indeed, supporting the idea of the real depth of design, Pye gives the example of the routine complexity an architect faces: 'all manner of different considerations will influence an architect's decisions about the shape he is to enclose, but the chief of them will always be the probable activities of the people' who use the space.[55] In other words, appropriate for product design, conceiving design problems is complex and geared to understanding people's needs in using whatever is being designed. Such functional requirements far outreach the single one of 'economy'. They refer to the idea of the fundamental, experiential depth of design. To confirm, Pye, I think, refers to this depth as 'useless'; and as a literary device against engineering design. So, such rhetorical usage perhaps does properly hint at the necessarily aesthetic nature of design grounded in rich conceptions of need and flourishing. With these ideas supporting that of 'function', design is understood in the light of people's experiential lives; and not merely as economy in production and a 'gets the job done' attitude.

As Roger Scruton has argued, it is useful then to turn to Ludwig Wittgenstein because he combines the functional and experiential in explaining our everyday aesthetic lives. I think that Wittgenstein's analysis of the fundamental nature of the aesthetic, especially how it operates experientially in our everyday lives, takes philosophical understanding of design beyond the either/or analyses and supposed dichotomies of function and appearance, engineering and styling, and science and art that still pervade it, and that Pye was addressing.

Wittgenstein observed that 'it is remarkable that in real life, when aesthetic judgements are made, aesthetic adjectives such as "beautiful", "fine", etc., play hardly any role at all'; rather 'the words you use are more akin to "right" and "correct"'.[56] Design teams carrying out user testing of their everyday products could doubtless make similar observations of the verbal responses of users to prototype products. In the same vein, typical everyday users of products do not possess any rules of design but would suggest improvements to products in terms akin to Wittgenstein's carpenter who, designing a door, looks at it and says: 'Higher, higher, higher ... oh, all right' (Gesture) (Fig. 1).[57] They are like, following another of Wittgenstein's examples, someone who knows a good suit and says: '"That's the right length", "That's too short", "That's too narrow"'.[58] And how does a user of a designed thing show approval? In ways akin to approval of a suit: 'chiefly by wearing it often, liking it when it is seen, etc.'[59] So, Wittgenstein concludes that 'perhaps the most important thing in connection with aesthetics is what may be called aesthetic reactions, e.g. discontent, disgust, discomfort'.[60]

Scruton draws conclusions about aesthetics in general and architectural aesthetics from Wittgenstein's observations and interpretations of everyday aesthetic experiences. So, Scruton rightly notes that Wittgenstein's focus is not on the arts 'but addresses instead the role of the aesthetic in everyday life'.[61] My purpose here is confined to showing how the observations apply (and where they do not) to the philosophical aesthetics of design. Indeed, I think they indicate that design work and using designed things epitomize the aesthetic in everyday life and play the largest part.

In the spirit of Wittgenstein, Scruton evokes this sense of everyday aesthetic life: 'You are *at work*, and if you stand back from time to time to look at the result it is not in order to enjoy a brief moment of disinterested contemplation but rather to see whether it is right,

Figure 1 Haus Wittgenstein, Vienna, 1926–29. Viennaslide / Alamy Stock Photo.

whether it fits, whether it is as it should be.'[62] Scruton continues, still after Wittgenstein, that the language 'when discussing it with your assistant, is normative – "too high", "too tight"'.[63] Apart from Scruton's quaint understanding of designers and their assistants, and the expressions likely to be used, the appeal is rightly to actual design work and its normative character. I do not pursue this via Scruton at this level though, since his next examples – 'laying a table, dressing for a party or a funeral, arranging your room, putting something on display, gardening' – betray an absence, despite the seeming presence of design work, of philosophic interest in the design and use of everyday products.[64] Rather, it is apposite to design to briefly pursue Scruton's view of the everyday aesthetics of architecture.

To reiterate, Scruton asks where entering the field of aesthetics via Wittgenstein – 'through studying . . . day-to-day attempts to make things "look right"' – takes us.[65] One result, at least, is aesthetic functionalism about architecture. As Andy Hamilton notes, Scruton's advocacy of that position 'treats function as the ground of aesthetic understanding of architecture'.[66] Moreover, 'for Scruton, the truth in functionalism is that one cannot abstract from one's knowledge of a building's utility in appreciating it aesthetically'.[67] Also, an aesthetics of architecture is an aesthetics of everyday life; architecture is aesthetic 'through and through'.[68]

A fundamental similarity between architecture and design work is evident in the centrality placed on function and its relation to the aesthetic. Scruton's architect or builder is like a designer in working impersonally to functional requirements set by buildings and products. And neither the builder nor the designer can adopt a self-consciously artistic attitude if their work is to meet the necessarily public demands set by buildings and things of general, everyday use. Rather, 'in being functional, it [the building] satisfies aesthetic criteria'.[69] But what does this mean for architecture, and perhaps by extension for design? The first thing to note is that Scruton does not argue that architecture's function is to produce aesthetic experiences. Certainly, the same is true of design. A designer is, first and foremost, charged with designing things that perform their designated function. Where then is the aesthetic in Scruton's aesthetic functionalism about architecture that might apply to design?

It helps to first remove one idea of aesthetic appreciation. In architectural appreciation, Scruton calls this 'sculpturalism'. 'Sculpturalism' is his term for the idea that architecture should be treated solely in virtue of its expressive, artistic values; but it gives its 'decorative aspect an unwarranted autonomy'.[70] This is akin to limiting design to issues of styling. I say more on this when constructing the 'design apology' from the statements designers make about the nature of their design work. But a taster is the American designer Raymond Loewy's comment that to understand design as limited to changing and appreciating the appearance of products would be to falsely reduce it to mere 'face-lift' work.[71] So, alongside Scruton's aesthetic functionalism about architecture, design's notion of the aesthetic is not a merely 'sculptural' or formal appreciation of things. This issue echoes Forsey's analysis of the aesthetic appreciation of coffee pots in terms of mere 'look' against an experiential description that includes our felt experiences while using things. Understanding the aesthetics of design, like architecture, appeals to all-round notions of aesthetic 'fit' and 'harmony' when using a product or building. It is with those aesthetic criteria in mind that aesthetic functionalism about architecture parallels aesthetic functionalism about design.

So, I do not pursue further Scruton's aesthetic functionalism except to note a false development of Wittgenstein's observations. That is the idea that 'the classical tradition [in architectural practice] is the natural result of taking aesthetic judgement seriously': that is, in the light of Wittgenstein's general remarks.[72] It is a curiosity in Scruton's overall analysis of the aesthetic given the seeming commitment to aesthetic judgements grounded in everyday experience rather than the application of preset aesthetic styles. That aside, there are no reasonable grounds at all for commitment to a single style in design work. In short, designers argue design solutions from design problems. Design problems are constructed from the functional requirements of things and places. The results are evidently various.[73] Edward Winters makes a similar point about Scruton's analysis and street architecture.[74] I share Winters's sense that while broadly agreeing with Scruton's Wittgenstein-inspired account of everyday aesthetic experience, there are good reasons to resist 'his prescriptions for architecture and the street'.[75] Winters argues on the basis that Scruton's classicism about architectural style condemns us to mere 'neatness', to 'the well-mannered street'.[76] More to the point, no single 'style' follows from an understanding of everyday aesthetic experience. Take Nairn's assessments of buildings and streets in London. Nairn can appreciate a curving Georgian crescent and a brutalist tower block with equal regard because he sees them working *in situ*, as well-designed buildings offering their solutions to the housing-design problems they each address.[77] Turning to design work, it is variegated across products, homes, and places, demanding attention to a broad range of functional requirements. It is perhaps the case that 'neatness' – Winters's bugbear – does have a greater say in those categories, to greater and lesser degrees. Still, the theoretic issue is that it is a matter, neatness or otherwise, resolved by the construal of design problems in every case. Nairn illustrates that point for places.

Conclusion

It is unsurprising, perhaps, given the absence of any coherent philosophy of design, and of one that accounts for what designers do, in terms both of design work's nature and range, that an editorial titled 'A Matter of Definitions' in the design journal *Disegno* admitted having 'no idea' how to answer the question 'what even is design?'[78] The admission was prompted by the seeming disconnected diversity of the contents of an issue that included the material history of silipol, gender in design, the restoration of Jesus's tomb, and porcelain tiling at London's Victoria & Albert Museum. Persevering but uncertain, the editor fixed on what they perceived as a common thread, namely that all are 'about how people have attempted to shape their environments'.[79] This albeit vague conclusion at least alludes to thinking about design in terms of its general value as an activity; and in turn that value is set in terms of people's everyday lives with products and in places. In that respect, it is a reasonable allusion to what Borgmann calls the 'depth of design'.

Borgmann's description of design work's profound aims and effects on everyday life counters any easy fallback on one or other basic intuition – scientific or artistic – about the essence of design. But within Design Studies this is too often misconstrued as suggesting design's moral and political work to improve the world, rather than the experiential improvements through better products and places – the kind of work design does which can be understood by aesthetic criteria. While Parsons and Forsey, in their detailed philosophical inquiries, nominally acknowledge the profundity of design, they both fail to address the work of designers and their statements about its general nature. The results, in both cases, are skewed and reduced views of design in terms of function and beauty, respectively. Thus, they misunderstand why design is important in our everyday lives. It is necessary to visit other areas of philosophical interest in design to begin to explain its true nature and significance. And in doing that, Scruton is right to suggest the help Wittgenstein offers about the everyday nature of aesthetic experience and value. Pye's apparent scepticism about design's essential functionalism is assuaged by this account, since it offers an expansive, experiential view of the functional in everyday life that includes design's so-called 'useless [aesthetic] work'.

In summary, the eclecticism and often political didacticism of Design Studies precludes it from focused philosophical analyses, although philosophical contributions like Borgmann's are important. Attempts so far at general philosophy of design have failed, falsely embedding design solely in either modernism (like Parsons's philosophy of design) or philosophical disputes about Kantian notions of beauty (like Forsey's aesthetics of design). Observations on the general nature of design work like Pye's and of its everyday aesthetic character like Wittgenstein's are, however, a promising path to a philosophical aesthetics of design. That route, to start, suggests the requirement to analyse what designers say about their work and thus identify the key concepts – and how they are understood by designers – that drive it. Broadly, I call that the 'design apology'.

2

Aesthetic functionalism about design

Introduction

All designers with a general interest in design work beyond their specialist area of design have stated, one way or another, in essays or interviews or manifestos, why they think design is important to the purpose and quality of human life. A metacritical approach based on philosophical analysis of these general statements by designers about the aims and value of their work establishes a general 'design apology'. Apologies answer questions like 'what makes design a good thing to have in one's life?' Designers couch their work in the prosaic terminology of 'need', 'function', and 'problem-solving'. But I shall argue that their 'apologies' for design work, while properly about human needs, are aims for design work conceived in aesthetic terms like 'fit', 'harmony', and 'good living'. So, they are properly understood within an account of aesthetic experience as an adaptive and consummatory experience. In short, when designers talk about the general value of design, they do so on the grounds that it delivers that kind of experience. Designers' apologies for design are essentially aesthetic defences of design.

The composite 'design apology' is therefore an aesthetic account of the value of design in our everyday lives and supports aesthetic functionalism about design. Aesthetic functionalism about design amounts to a cluster of aesthetic criteria around meeting user needs for products of everyday use in ways that improve life, adding things of functionally aesthetic value and creating built environments and communities that aid the good life. From the design apology, we can adduce that design work has several key components of, I will argue, connected philosophical interest, namely need, function, flourishing, aesthetic experience, and value. Indeed, thinking about design work in these terms, the 'design apology' contributes to the philosophy of need, taking understanding of fundamental human needs beyond the idea of 'vital need' and associated political rights and action.

The 'design apology'

The purpose of design, set by the UK Design Council, is 'to make life better by design'.[1] It further characterizes design and states its mission with these statements:

> Design shapes the world. Design turns ideas into reality, whether it's a place, product, service or the systems that underpin how we live our lives. Design is a creative pursuit to make lives better. It uses creativity to collaboratively solve problems, reimagine and propose new ways of living. Design is a critical enabler of innovation and drives industry. It turns ideas into action.[2]

Additionally, the Council sets design work in an ecological context: 'Design for Planet means designing in a way that is good for our planet, and it sits at the heart of the Design Council's mission.'[3] Some quotes from designers on design are enlisted in support. Steve Jobs, the co-founder of Apple states that: 'Design is not just what it looks like and feels like. Design is how it works.' Bruce Mau, Canadian designer, innovator, educator, and author of Massive Change says: 'The fundamental idea of design is to make the world a better place.' Robert L. Peters, Canadian graphic designer and educator asserts that: 'Design creates culture. Culture shapes values. Values determine the future.'[4]

In these and the UK Design Council's overall aims and values, it is evident that design is understood by those within the design profession to extend out from designing products of everyday use to creating better places to live and work in, even to shaping whole cultures and managing the global environment. And within those broad normative aims, design work is essentially a problem-solving activity connected to industrial scale production of products, places, and systems of everyday living.

Examples of how these overarching aims – normative and functional – apply at product level come from the criteria applied to good designs. Nominations for the 2016 UK Design Museum's Designs of the Year were chosen based on four criteria. These criteria indicated both core functional demands and normative values, sometimes within a single criterion. So, for example, 'design that promotes or delivers change, from using new materials or processes to enabling new ways of living'; or 'design that enables access from a website offering an excellent user experience to design that will improve lives'.[5] Designs are merited within categories, that is, the types of design problems they engage (architectural, digital, transport, and so on), and how they then best solve them in specific instances (a housing estate, a government website, a city tram) within overall criteria strongly related to general norms of 'good living'. Such ideas synchronize with the aims and values of academic departments supporting the design profession's work. For example, the University Buffalo's School of Architecture and Planning includes a Centre for Inclusive Design and Environmental Access that promotes 'Universal Design': 'Universal design (UD) is a design process that enables and empowers a diverse population by improving human performance, health and wellness, and social participation.'[6]

These contemporary claims for design are far-reaching and ambitious. Perhaps such claims only represent our current concerns, especially cultural and environmental ones. Yet at the core of them are grand apologies for design that are themselves centred on fundamental concepts and ideas. And these are evident throughout the history of design thinking and work.

In that vein, when Charles and Ray Eames were interviewed after lifetimes in design and were asked 'what are the boundaries of design', they replied: 'what are the boundaries of problems'.[7] In the same interview asked about the primary condition for the practice of design and for its propagation, the reply was simply 'a recognition of need'.[8] Setting design in terms of solving problems of human needs is fundamental. Again, asked about to whom design addresses itself, the answer did not specify groups or numbers or classes but was that 'design addresses itself to the need'.[9] It has been rightly concluded that the Eameses thus 'saw design not as the pursuit of originality for its own sake but as a process of thinking about problems and their connection to surrounding historical, social and technological conditions'.[10] Specifically, in their mid-twentieth-century conditions, their objective was 'the simple thing of getting the best to the greatest number of people for the least [price]'.[11]

The basic elements of an Eameses' design apology – need, everyday things, mass production, affordability, quality – echo those of Anthony Bertram in the UK earlier in the century. His series of twelve radio talks on the BBC in 1937 were concerned with 'design as it affects people of incomes below £8 a week – that is, the vast majority'.[12] Moreover, 'good design is not a matter merely of wealth, much less of the chic, the latest thing'; it is a matter of 'the production of houses and goods which will best satisfy the needs of the people; their need of useful, honest, cheap, lasting and beautiful things to use and see in their everyday lives'.[13]

And moving to the twenty-first century, these basic elements of good design are expressed by IKEA. The foreword to a UK Design Museum exhibition in 2018, *Home Futures*, sponsored by IKEA was an opportunity for the company, through the curator of its museum, to state its design principles.[14] They are general enough, sharing much with all design principles, about needs and problem-solving, to warrant quoting fully. So, for IKEA at least:

> people's needs are quite similar over space and time, regardless of where we live . . . we interview thousands of people in their homes around the globe . . . [getting] an insight into people's needs, struggles and longings. We use this research to come up with new solutions to everyday puzzles. Our Democratic Design principles . . . state that all products in our range must be affordable, socially and environmentally sustainable, have beautiful form, long lasting quality and, finally, great functionality.[15]

To summarize the design apology thus far: design is concerned with identifying people's basic needs, solving design problems associated with them, and with designing products for mass production at affordable prices for customers. An added twenty-first-century dimension is that these aims are met within the constraints of environmental sustainability. On hold, I concede, is that this yet amounts to an essentially aesthetic set of criteria for good design.

Still, it is evident from these basic design aims – from sources like the Eames in America, Bertram's early attempts to advance mass, early modernist design in the UK, and from Scandinavian design principles – that it is a short step to the larger claims of design necessarily having goals associated with generating improved, good, everyday lives. This can be couched in ethical terms. Asked 'is there a design ethic?', Charles Eames replied that 'there are always design constraints, and these often imply an ethic'.[16] Good designs respond to real needs and these needs are typically complex and never austerely functional. A 'design ethic' or apology is evident in Charles Eames's advice to students in the Eames Office, including 'avoid the pat answer – the formula'; 'avoid the preconceived idea'; 'study objects made in the past, recent and ancient, but never without the technological and social conditions responsible'; 'search out the true need, physical and psychological'; and, 'art is the way you do your work'.[17] Eames confirms that the design apology's concept of need is not a consumerist one; designers should identify real needs and work accordingly.

The 'waste makers' analysis noted in the Introduction suggests some designers, at least, must have only ever paid lip service to the design apology's insistence on only designing products that were solutions to problems set by real needs. Yet, figurehead and leading American designers like Henry Dreyfuss and Raymond Loewy, at the apogee of American consumerism in the mid-twentieth century, still lauded simplicity, efficiency, and happiness as core design concepts. The experiential standard of 'fit', of real needs well met, is developed by Dreyfuss when he sets out tenets or a mission for industrial design. These are that design centres on people as users of things and that in that relation there is either 'friction' – failed design – or success, indicated by a product being 'safe, comfortable and efficient to use, and being attractive to buy and giving a sense of happiness'.[18] Ergonomic features are explicable in terms of a product meeting its functional requirements *per se*; but the appeal to attractiveness and happiness are additional normative functional requirements also cohering around concerns with 'fit' and experiential 'rightness'. Dreyfuss's design apology begins to indicate how meeting real needs for products appeals to aesthetic notions after Wittgenstein's descriptions and analysis noted in Chapter 1.

Similarly, Loewy's design apology is worded as an industrial designer's theory of aesthetics: 'it would seem that more than function itself, simplicity is the deciding factor in the aesthetic equation. One might call the [design] process beauty through function and simplification.'[19] Loewy might be viewed as the epitome of post–World War II American consumer culture; yet, for him, design is not a mere 'face-lift' job.[20] In other words: 'good design is not an applied veneer'.[21] Moreover, by the 1970s Loewy reflected on 'phoney designers' who 'flooded' markets with 'cheap, sleazy junk bought by consumers who saw gaudiness as a mark of advanced futuristic design'.[22] He decries a 'neon civilization' and 'plastic world' echoing the earlier recognition of the 'the waste makers' by Packard as being at the heart of the problem of design.[23]

The 'design ethic' recognized by Eames is, then, evidenced in *aesthetic* terms by Dreyfuss's and Loewy's appeals to the felt and visible in good design. Well-designed products are comfortable in use and simple in their look, in contrast to phoney designs, the merely 'gaudy' making false visual appeals to meeting 'modern needs'. Loewy further reflected after fifty years as an industrial designer that his earlier design apology was perhaps facile. That which had stated that 'industrial design keeps the customer happy, his client in the black, and the designer busy'.[24] Left as such, it is indeed a design apology that legitimizes wasteful design and production. Still, it 'may seem facile, but one can infer from it . . . a concern for the society, for those who have the responsibility to initiate and produce, and for the profession of industrial design to be understood and involved'.[25] So, Loewy concluded, 'don't further complicate life', and that design should elevate 'the aesthetic level of society'.[26]

This increasing sophistication of the design apology – developing its concerns with real needs, affordable products, and personal experience, toward the aesthetic quality of life across the board – finds fuller expression in the German designer Dieter Rams, best known for his twentieth-century designs for Braun and his '10 Principles of Good Design'.[27] These fundamental design principles for products relate to a more general set of aims for the natural environment and humanity. So, for example, one principle explicitly states that 'Good design is eco-friendly: Design makes an important contribution to the preservation of the environment. It conserves resources and minimises physical and visual pollution throughout the lifecycle of the product.'[28] Together with 'Good design is as little design as possible', with its 'less, but better' and 'back to simplicity' calls, these two principles clearly chime with the ecological concerns raised by the 'waste age'.

Moreover, the ecological principles are related to a holistic view of the role of designed things in our everyday lives. Rams's ecological principle is expressed not only in terms of managing natural resources but also evokes the idea of 'visual pollution'. This might as easily be proposed as an aesthetic principle. It is not dissimilar to Nairn's outrage at the visual pollution of street furniture noted when outlining the general 'problem of design'. Still, Rams does propose that 'Good design is aesthetic ... because products we use every day affect our person and our well-being'.[29] Of course, function is still at the fore: 'Good design makes a product useful.'[30] With these functional, ecological, and aesthetic principles in mind, Rams concludes that design is concerned with 'less and less': that is, with using fewer natural resources and producing less rubbish.[31] More significantly, in terms of the construction of a general design apology, Rams is convinced, therefore, that 'there is an ethics of design'.[32] He claims that 'Designers are critics of civilization, critics of technology, critics of society,' no less.[33]

Rams believes his whole approach to design work amounts 'philosophically, [to creating] a world that people could live in'; and just 'living with what you need'.[34] So, naturally, design work continues beyond criticism. Designers 'have to keep trying to create something new that emerges from the criticism'.[35] And this introduces a final key element of Rams's design apology. That is the idea that designs help create not just a felt sense of well-being and an attractive, uncluttered built environment but facilitate our ability to lead creative lives ourselves. So, 'a shaver or a chair, a film camera or a shelf should have the objective usefulness of tools ... They should help people to solve small or large problems. They should help them to be creative themselves. They should live with them and enable them to become friends.'[36] From well-designed shavers and shelves to self-expression and friendship? Perhaps it is explicable in terms of another of Rams's design principles: 'Good design is unobtrusive. Products fulfilling a purpose are like tools. They are neither decorative objects nor works of art. Their design should therefore be both neutral and restrained, to leave room for the user's self-expression.'[37] Similarly, this time perhaps explaining how friendship might follow good design: 'Design is not just about the formal design of our *Dingwelt*, our "world of things"; it determines the life of every individual and how we all live with one another.'[38]

The design apology, with Rams's principles, has come a long way from meeting needs for functional things at affordable prices. And yet the core ideas remain constant. In that vein, a recent general introduction describes all design's 'shared interest in improving society'; its necessarily 'optimistic and forward-looking' approach; and its aspiration to make humans stronger, more adept, and able to manage their environment. Good design meets human needs in ways that improve lives. Rams reflects then that he has one 'primary insight': 'less but better.'[39] That should make all designers of any design ask: does it 'enrich our lives or does it only appeal to ideas of status?'; moreover, 'does the new product dominate me?'[40] So, the goal of 'less if better' is to allow *our* lives to flourish: good design is 'a willingness for order – for simple, calm, restrained forms with longer, more aesthetic, useful lives.'[41] What changes then within the design apology is the scope and complexity of the concept of human need. And what is notable is the idea that richer, complex notions of need and human functioning refer to ideas about aesthetic experience and value. They can therefore be understood independently of what Rams, and to a lesser extent Charles Eames, back to Bertram too, think of as ethical demands placed on design work to improve our everyday lives. I consider the concept of need in aesthetic terms in the section entitled 'Need, function, flourishing'. Before that, I want to round off the design apology with the important and related contributions of modernist and Japanese thinking about design.

Charlotte Perriand's career in design spanned most of the twentieth century and its development is representative of the design apology's evolution over that period. It marks its enrichment from the predominance of an austerely functional modernism and creating the 'new man' to ideas about simple, beautiful functionality embracing Japanese philosophical insights about design and spiritual well-being. In the 1920s, at the height of Le Corbusier's and modernism's so-called 'machine aesthetic', Perriand's design apology is written in the style of a futurist manifesto with bold claims about designs for the life of the 'NEW MAN' of the twentieth century, including 'what is his house to be?'[42] From there, design problems are deduced: hygiene, tidiness, rest, beds, chairs, and tables. And so, 'We have stated the problem; now we must solve it'.[43] Although ostensibly about choosing metal over wood as a design material, together with leather, marble, and glass, 'Wood or Metal?' is notable as a whole apology for design, asserting that good design produces 'a range of wonderful combinations and new aesthetic effects', 'a new lyric beauty' even. The piece ends with an aim, presumably thought to be delivered by good design work: 'We must keep morally and physically fit'.[44] The connections between materials, design, beauty, and moral fitness are implicit but unexplained. Does using a modernist chez longue keep us morally fit as well as relaxed?

Still, it is important to note here in the context of constructing the design apology that modernism's and Perriand's concern is fundamentally with how we live our everyday lives. And that is thought to necessarily engage a richer notion of what good design achieves. As Mary McLeod states: 'Perriand wanted her furniture and interior spaces to be more than just functional or aesthetically innovative; she hoped to help people achieve an integrated harmonious existence'.[45] And: 'she wanted to create spaces, organizations, and even utopian schemes that encouraged the collective transformation of daily existence: her objective was personal fulfilment for *all*'.[46]

In 1935, Perriand contended that modern designers 'intend to demonstrate ... that the problem of the family house is above all a problem of social order'.[47] By 1950, however, the terms of the design problem for dwellings had altered to a concern with its 'art'. This does not represent a contradiction in Perriand's apology though. In the 1935 article, Perriand had outlined a history of human development and corresponding types of suitable dwelling, noting that peasants raising livestock required something different to modern, urban man. Later, Perriand acknowledges that there is more to the design problems associated with housing than acquiring the latest domestic appliances.[48] Perriand expressed this as the idea that the solution to modern living was not realized 'through "equipment" alone': 'dwellings should be designed not only to satisfy material specifications; they should also create conditions that foster a harmonious balance and spiritual freedom in people's lives'.[49]

This development of Perriand's design apology openly acknowledges a debt to the Japanese philosophy of living expressed in 'Teaism'.[50] Its ideas are neatly expressed by her in the statement that 'the ambience of our dwellings should foster calm, relaxation, harmony'.[51] Perriand had been brought to Japan in 1940 to advise their manufacturing companies, where she was assisted by Sori Yanagi, later a well-known designer in his own right. Here she also witnessed Japanese craft-industry ideas and tradition. Supposed opposing ideas and practices of machines and handcraft, of modern development and tradition, and of things and lives, became twinned in Perriand's development of the design apology. So, for her, the core concern with good design of everyday objects at affordable prices, available in department stores, remains in 1950 but for a kind of life, rather than just practical urban existence: good design, in short, reflects 'a philosophy of sorts'.[52] Perriand's work in Japan included organizing exhibitions of good design which included affordable and available products, from baskets and saucepans to light switches. These exhibitions aimed to educate the public in the possibilities of the beauty of things of everyday use. Perriand's thoughts on art and the everyday closely resemble those of William Morris from the 1870s on 'the beauty of life' – that where there is form, there is the possibility of art – when she stated that 'there is art in everything, whether it be an action, a vase, a saucepan, a glass, a piece of sculpture, a jewel, a way of being.'[53]

So, Perriand's later design apology extended the ideas of 1920s modernism, of which she was also a key part, to a more rounded 'philosophy of life', drawing on Japanese traditions of making and living. Design was also afforded a didactic purpose, educating ordinary consumers of the living, experiential benefits of good design. These characteristics of the design apology are fully evident in the statements and work of Kenya Hara. He is described as 'a designer of designers' and, among many pursuits and activities, is the art director of MUJI and president of the Nippon Design Center, as well as heading his own design company.[54] Hara is also said to have always had an interest in 'design's philosophical underpinnings'.[55] So, his statements are worth noting; indeed, I quote them at some length as they represent a full expression of the design apology.

Perhaps his most striking claim is that 'Design is a gentle education that influences the quality of desire.'[56] The claim is made on these grounds:

> Products and environments are harvests reaped from the soil of human desire. To create quality products and environments, we have to actualize well-fertilized soil by refining human desire. Design is fundamental to the process. Interacting with well-thought-out design induces an awakening from which changes in our desires arise, resulting in modifications to patterns of consumption, resource allocation, and finally, lifestyle.[57]

So, 'The essence of design is to make visible underlying potential and reveal an explicit, significant path for the future, to clearly delineate a vision that can be shared with many.'[58] In more concrete terms, Hara applies his design apology to 'the future of fabrication and manufacturing' in Japan with its socio-economic situation in mind: his design solutions lay emphasis on problems related to tourism and hospitality, competing with more industrialized nations, and an ageing population.[59]

To reiterate, Hara's personal philosophy of design represents the fullest expression of the design apology in terms of the range of terms used to describe design work and by the wide scope of its design aims.[60] Design educates our aesthetic sensibilities which in turn determine our choices of products. Good designs improve our lives. They also determine how things should be produced. And good design extends to designing products and places that enhance the cultural and economic life of a nation. These are elements of the design apology that are noted in, for example, Loewy's idea of design shaping American culture and similar 'nation and culture-building' ideas have been expressed for Scandinavian design. Indeed, writing a preface to the English Edition of *Designing Japan* Hara considers his design apology to be of global interest.[61] It is a reasonable claim. For example, The *Harvard Design Magazine* devoted an issue in 2021 to 'America', with articles examining 'the prevailing notion of America as a concept, as a culture, as a country, and as a state of mind'.[62]

It should be noted that while the design apology is not couched in overtly moral or political terms, its aims are clearly normative. Its aims all lie within an overarching aim of 'improved lives'. So, it is useful to end with an example of the design apology at its fullest addressing a set of real design problems. Hara suggests that good design will help Japan tackle the demographic and social issues of an ageing society. In the UK the Royal College of Art's 'Design Age Institute' aims to 'help people age happier . . . through the transformative power of design'.[63] It works with designers and businesses to develop products to that end. So, simply put, design is evidently interested in needs associated with products but also with happiness. The paucity of thinking about design work in terms of mere function or style or beauty – failing to understand the full 'depth of design' in Borgmann's phrase – is therefore exposed by the design apology constructed here, and perhaps no more than by such work. I turn then to the fundamental philosophical concept at issue, revealed by the design apology: need.

Need, function, flourishing

At the outset, I suggested that the general 'problem of design' might be best examined holistically in the context of human function *per se* rather than through a piecemeal examination of the functional requirements of things. And the 'design apology' shows that designers indeed think likewise (as well as designing things), evident in the common use of key terms like 'needs', 'function', and terms clustered around happiness and flourishing that depend on good design.

So, the example of how designers work with an idea of need and the design problems associated with ageing is worth pursuing because it illustrates similarities and differences with philosophical notions of need. Jeremy Myerson notes how in the 1980s designers couched the needs of the elderly in limited clinical and utilitarian terms. Design was exclusively concerned with alleviating medical conditions with functional design for things to help with cooking and bathing, for example.[64] Now, Myerson notes, design's understanding of ageing is 'broader and richer'; so also therefore are design problems and solutions. Design aims to support 'social interaction and personal productivity'.[65] It is a reminder of John Stuart Mill's famous dictum in argument against utilitarian thinking that there is more to the good life than being a 'satisfied pig'. In other words, the twentieth-century approach to designing products for the elderly reflected a merely scientific functionalism about design. Products were not designed with richly experiential aims, happiness, in mind; designers worked with a minimal view of need.

The example indicates three things, that I will now examine, about design and the idea of need. They are: (a) the idea of need in good design work is not equivalent to that in the philosophy of need, where the latter aims to establish a concept of 'vital need' to protect or ensure the rights of individuals against 'aggregate thinking'; (b) the philosophy of need does, however, provide related notions that do accord to design work, especially in discussions about how needs relate to broader ideas of human flourishing; and (c) the idea that design work is essentially where everyday human needs are tested. In that regard, I argue that good designers are exemplary general, everyday 'needs-meeters'.

In the context of design and 'vital need', it is apposite to use David Wiggins's analysis of need since it is grounded in his personal involvement with planners building roads through London in the 1960s. The experience highlighted for him that notions of need, vital need, and desires were not ones that could be taken for granted.[66] Wiggins felt there was something wrong with the aggregative reasoning that was used to evaluate schemes: why did they exclude the deprivation of vital needs from proper consideration? Such schemes to build urban motorways seemed to him to destroy parts of the 'close-knit social and urban fabric of London'.[67] Against this background outside of formal philosophy, Wiggins saw a philosophical requirement for a notion of need that would act as a constraint on such reasoning that put the aggregated value of time saved by travelling on new urban routes against the effect on the individual lives of ordinary citizens whose homes would be demolished in the process. These citizens had 'vital needs' that should be protected: they were needs that are 'grave, deeply entrenched and scarcely substitutable. They were things that mattered extremely'.[68] So, Wiggins developed a 'Limitation Principle' that it is unjust to sacrifice one person's vital need for the desires of many.[69] Wiggins thinks limitation principles like that are what the idea of need would entail for politics and public policy if taken seriously. It is worth noting, in that regard, that Wiggins also thinks that taking vital needs seriously is important in environmental questions, where the vital needs of human life itself are at stake: so, policies should not be entertained that risk that which is or will be necessary to human life against 'the hope of acquiring the superfluous i.e. that of which we have no vital need'.[70]

The design apology establishes that designers base their work on needs. The issue at stake is whether the concept of special 'vital needs', and the related 'limitation principle', properly has any role, theoretically and practically, in understanding the design apology. At its simplest expression, the straightforward answer is 'no': product designs, particularly, do not resolve on 'grave' vital needs but are about considering user needs associated with specific design problems. Designers work to meet needs and good design work adopts practices in which unmet needs are identified. As such, no limitation principle applies.[71] Design presupposes problems of need that require solving. Yet it is in that general presupposition that a further philosophical notion of need is important to fully understanding the design apology. That is the idea of human flourishing. While designs do not typically involve questions of *protecting* vital needs, they are more likely to encounter questions about the nature of human flourishing.[72]

The explanation of 'needs' in *The Oxford Companion to Philosophy* provides a simple equation between needs and flourishing: 'an organism's needs are what it requires to live the normal life of its kind – flourishing rather than merely surviving'.[73] It is an appeal too to the Aristotelian framework of understanding human life functionally and in turn in terms of needs and happiness. But as Alfred Edward Taylor states, considering Aristotle's account, it is one thing to answer that 'happiness' is the best kind of life for an individual member of society but 'the real problem is one of fact. What kind of life deserves to be called happiness?'[74] Still, Taylor argues that the answer lies in the work or function of man, in some life 'which can *only* be lived by man'; in a life at the very least that takes it beyond 'feeding and growing' since these are common to all organisms.[75] Also sympathetic to Aristotle, the moral philosopher Philippa Foot argues that a basic idea of need and human function grounds what a good life is: 'There is the fact that a certain network of interrelated concepts such as *function* and *purpose* is found where there is evaluation of all kinds of living things, including human beings.'[76] And in all cases, including human beings, 'it seems significant that there is a special *form* of explanation – teleological explanation – to which the idea of function and purpose is related'.[77] She argues that questions about why certain things are done have satisfactory answers placing these in the life of the species.

Soran Reader's analysis of Aristotle on needs concludes that while reasonably using an everyday concept of necessity, Aristotle in fact identifies the wrong set of human needs as proper parts of human life. Aristotle's list includes 'warcraft, political judgement, and priesthood' and excludes the ordinary necessities of food, arts and crafts, trading, and working 'on the grounds that they are ignoble and inimical to virtue'.[78] Reader also suggests that meeting ordinary human needs is a 'good in itself', thus meeting the Aristotelian demand for what constitutes a 'proper part'. This suggestion leads to considerations about whether the good designer, working to the design apology, therefore best meets Reader's Aristotelian requirements of a 'good needs-meeter'.[79] But, before that, what are the proper parts of human life? Answering will help assess the role of designers.

As a matter of fact, basic human needs for food, clothing, and shelter are a given and indeed created proto-design work. Peter Kropotkin's *The Conquest of Bread* might be taken as a case study in the historical development of the idea of human needs 'after bread has been secured'.[80] Once our basic needs are met then the demand is: 'the Right to Well-Being: Well-Being for all!'[81] The idea of well-being opens a Pandora's box of claims of need and about the best means to meet them. Following Kropotkin, a little further, it might be generally agreed that there is a need to remove domestic drudgery from lives.

That in turn encourages thinking about designing gadgets that will meet that need. Kropotkin argues that and more though; he argued for the need for luxury:

> Man is not a being whose exclusive purpose in life is eating, drinking, and providing a shelter for himself . . . [O]ther needs . . . of an artistic character, will thrust themselves forward. These needs are of the greatest variety; they vary with each and every individual; and the more society is civilized, the more will individuality be developed, and the more will desires be varied.[82]

For Kropotkin, at least, luxury denotes 'artistic pleasure' and not 'the foolish and ostentatious display of the bourgeois class'.[83] Kropotkin knew William Morris and writes in a similar vein about art and the everyday, similarly evoking ideas about the aesthetic experience and value afforded by well-made things of everyday use, of 'art' outside of fine art and its making and appreciation. So, after Morris, 'art' involves 'pictures, optical instruments, luxurious furniture, artistic jewellery': 'the many things'.[84] Kropotkin includes 'Sevres china and a velvet dress' as conceivably real needs.[85] Again, entirely in the spirit of Morris's design work and aims, he states that 'everything that surrounds man, in the street, in the interior and exterior of public monuments, must be of pure artistic form'.[86] Those interested in their homes too would engage in artistic associations that embellish them.

These ideas of needs of 'luxury' have a twofold significance for understanding the fullest expressions of the design apology. Design's pursuance of needs is not restricted to meeting basic needs. Additionally, luxurious needs are explicable in terms of Borgmann's depth of design being related to our full active engagement with designed things. In other words, such needs rely, properly, on notions of the necessity of aesthetic experience and value, of 'artistic pleasure'. When luxury goods are experienced by those who are involved in their making and real use, they become needs that good design meets.

Kropotkin gives the example of the grand piano. It is a need for those who play the piano, enjoy its playing, or those who are skilled at making them.[87]

To reiterate, Kropotkin's view is interesting because it suggests something like Borgmann's idea that design's depth is evident when it provokes our active engagement with designed things. Kropotkin surely alludes to the depth of design being a function of its aesthetic depth, to it affording the possibilities of aesthetic experience and value in everyday life. This 'depth' is what is properly called 'luxury' too. And that some luxury goods are deemed needs because they enhance aesthetic lives supports a view that good designers work toward general human flourishing.

The need for luxury in this sense is noted by Sudjic as the need for 'quality' in design. He notes that luxury isn't necessarily 'the compulsion to acquire too much too fast'; it 'had other meanings in the past'.[88] Putting the accuracy (or otherwise) of the history aside, Sudjic is making a general point about luxury and design that resonates with Kropotkin's aims for meeting needs that allow us to flourish through things of luxury when he argues that it 'used to be the respite that mankind found for itself from the daily struggle for survival. It was the pleasure to be found in understanding the quality of material things that were thoughtfully and carefully made.'[89] In that quality we share the maker's pleasure, says Sudjic. So, we share not just a tactile sensation but something of the maker's design work and intelligence. Sudjic evokes an idea of aesthetic experience as both a felt experience and a critical one. I have more to say on the nature of aesthetic experience and its relation to value in the section entitled 'Aesthetic experience and value'; but Sudjic's observation is important in prompting thoughts about what real luxury in design consists of and how it relates to the kind of experience that is both properly aimed at by designers and enjoyed by users. It helps distinguish the kind of luxury that Kropotkin notes after Morris from the diamond-encrusted laptops that irk Sudjic.[90] It should also help expose the 'the occult language of initiates' that Sudjic also disparagingly notes.[91]

Before that and in the light of the normativity and richness of human needs, and that designers must design things that meet these needs, I return to Reader's suggestion 'that the Aristotelian good man will necessarily be a good needs-meeter' because 'meeting ordinary needs is difficult'.[92] A cautionary note on whether designers fulfil this role is made by Christian Madsbjerg.[93] He criticizes standard 'design thinking' that there is only one design principle, namely 'convenience': it means ordinary people are treated as 'idiots'.[94] The upshot are people 'not able to figure out how to use anything, how to do anything'.[95] To illustrate, he gives the example of flat elevators in airports to move people around: 'we don't even have to walk anymore'.[96] Madsbjerg argues this state of affairs is the product of UX (user experience) design work that only provides 'very, very flat descriptions of us' and correspondingly 'boring' designs.[97] He contrasts this 'user need' model with a time when 'designs used to be about creating an aesthetic vision'.[98] Instead design now works toward producing what he terms 'sickening nice' in products and places.[99] So that 'everything looks the same today'.[100]

It is hardly a description supportive of the idea that design work might be the place where human needs are really tested and determined. And that, therefore, designers be elevated to the status of exemplary needs-meeters. Madsbjerg does not give up that idea though: he suggests that designers abandon or at least limit their 'user experience' view of testing designs for more long-standing thinking about human beings reflected in anthropology, sociology, and philosophy. I think the aesthetic understanding of the design apology suggests that a more specific theoretic discipline be referred to, namely philosophical aesthetics with due attention also to ideas from the philosophy of need about human flourishing. Certainly, the design apology in the light of aesthetic experience and the depth that offers in meeting needs accords with Madsbjerg's concerns of a design apology misunderstood in the limited terms of convenience and UX testing.

Still, needs do not present themselves *a priori*. Rather, good design work shows that needs are selected from our experiences using things. This is not an arbitrary or 'useless' process, though, nor one based solely on designing convenience, but properly a careful selection based on well-conceived design problems and on aesthetic experiences and evaluations of design solutions. Another way to put this is to claim that designers test flourishing in terms of the aesthetic experience and value of the things and places they design. Returning to Wiggins's example of urban planning: think of 'modern transport planners' habit of speaking of "mobility" (by car) as a standing need of western civilization'.[101] We can replace 'mobility' with any contemporary term, like 'connectivity' for example. Wiggins points out that economic and social developments might make that a short or medium term 'need' with some 'entrenchment' (in the example, if local facilities close, then 'mobility' by car is needed). 'But, if alternative tendencies can be envisaged, we shall get a fairer view of all the available options if we realise that the right name for *the standing, invariable need* [my italics] (the need that underlies the shorter term need) is not "mobility" but, more plastically and indefinitely, "access [to facilities that are frequently needed]"'.[102] Given this analysis, establishing needs in design seems to require precisely what Wiggins calls (for establishing rights anyway) an *a posteriori* consensual approach.[103] By working with felt responses to using products and places, with flourishing in mind, good designers indeed adopt this approach as a matter of course. Conceiving design problems and solutions only in terms of presupposed needs and their purely functional requirements is akin to the destructive planning solutions in Wiggins's example of urban planning.

Good design is exemplary 'needs-meeting' because needs are tested and met experientially. The design apology is cast in terms of testing design solutions to problems of need against felt experiences of fit and harmony and even happiness. But to confirm this understanding of meeting needs in the design apology, it is therefore also necessary to confirm the very possibility of everyday aesthetic experience and value in our engagement with things and places of everyday use. Only then can aesthetic functionalism about design be considered.

Aesthetic experience and value

Until recently, philosophical aesthetics was generally thought demarcated solely by a type of experience we have listening to music, reading poetry, looking at paintings, extending to our experiences of scenes in nature. This aesthetic experience was supposed to be of a distinctive emotional and contemplative character; and with an associated special vocabulary of aesthetic concepts, exclusively applied to them. Furthermore, such appreciation of art is set apart from our non-aesthetic everyday, practical lives, characterized as without the complexity and intensity required of true aesthetic experience. Such an understanding clearly precludes design from aesthetic appreciation and evaluation and must be addressed if aesthetic functionalism about design is to have any grounds. I do so here by presenting, descriptively, a general view of aesthetic experience and value that embraces both art and non-art activities, including making and using designed things. I do so, however, without directly engaging the theoretic issues that are then raised. I do that in Chapter 3, which deals with the idea of everyday aesthetics that has emerged from aesthetic theories of aspects of everyday life. Accounts of everyday aesthetics like those of Yuriko Saito and Sherri Irvin raise issues about whether any object or situation is capable of aesthetic experience. About whether aesthetic experience is in fact a divided notion between art and the everyday. And about the relation of everyday aesthetic experience to aesthetic value.

For now, the general issue of art and non-art philosophical aesthetics is neatly addressed by Robert Stecker: 'What possesses aesthetic value? According to a broad view, it can be found almost anywhere. According to a narrower view, it is found primarily in art and is applied to other items by courtesy of sharing some of the properties that make artworks aesthetically valuable.'[104] At the centre of any non-art aesthetic theory in Western philosophical aesthetics at least is John Dewey's account of aesthetic experience in *Art as Experience*. Dewey explains aesthetic experience as an adaptive encounter with things. Aesthetic experience has a distinctive phenomenology, which Dewey describes as a rhythmic 'movement' and 'consummation'. Such experience, which he calls 'an experience', means that we talk about *that* meal and *that* encounter, and the like.[105] For Dewey a 'consummation' of an experience does not simply represent the fact that a job is well done, a problem solved: just to do this could involve no more than checking that certain rules and regulations had been followed. In aesthetic experiences, there is a feeling that things are 'just so'. This feeling of 'harmony' or 'rightness' that can come in our experience of things is a feature basic to our aesthetically experiencing them. The feeling is generated by a 'movement' also basic to human life. This 'movement' of aesthetic experience is set by the biological demands of being a 'live creature': 'so while man is other than bird or beast, he shares basic vital functions with them and has to make the same basal adjustments if he is to continue the process of living'.[106] Dewey also talks in terms of harmony: the 'outer harmony' of integrating with our environment. This is a necessary condition of a sense of the 'inner harmony' attained when terms are made with it. Dewey thus talks about 'a mutual adaptation of the self and the object', of experiences coming to a close, where the closure 'is a felt harmony'.[107]

Dewey's account of aesthetic experience does not preclude non-art experiences. All our actions are capable of the adaptive qualities

Dewey associates with aesthetic experience.[108] Of relevance to design, aesthetic experiences accompany our creative work making things. Such works are not limited to 'high art' but include 'dance, song, utensils, and articles of daily living'.[109] All, including designed things, contribute to 'the life of a civilization'; indeed, they are its 'manifestation, record and celebration'.[110] Dewey's account of aesthetic experience thus accords with the design apology in two respects. One, the account resonates with design work, especially its general rhythm or pattern of assessing human needs and assessing design solutions against aesthetic criteria around a notion of fit. Two, a Deweyan account of aesthetic experience as a live encounter with value supports the general idea that design work legitimately aims at improving our everyday experiential lives. Offering just one example from design work here, the American designer Dreyfuss noted the 'friction' of poor design marking its failure to deliver a product that works: it evidently accords with Dewey's account of non-aesthetic experiences which are 'incomplete and inchoate' and mark failures to properly adapt.[111] And one theoretic example from the philosophy of need supporting the aesthetic phenomenology of successful design: Foot is surely right to acknowledge that Wiggins makes a valid point about the requirement that feelings accompany the right operations of human function and flourishing.[112]

Conclusion

The design apology conveys a rich and complex view of human needs. It sets aims for design accordingly. Design, in its fullest expression, aims at experiential flourishing – fit, harmony, well-being – in our everyday lives through well-designed things and places of use. Examination of the design apology in terms of needs, function, and flourishing reveals that successful, good design is marked by aesthetic experience and value. This warrants the aims of design in theory and practice so that good designers are rightly classed as 'needs-meeters' generating our aesthetic lives. This all amounts to aesthetic functionalism about design. How this plays out in different areas of design work – products, homes, cities – is the broad subject of Part II. Before that, I examine the philosophical idea of everyday aesthetics, its conceptions of experience and value, and the aims it sets, in the light of this analysis of design.

3

Design and aesthetics of the everyday

Introduction

In his introduction to the aesthetics of the everyday, Crispin Sartwell notes that 'everyday aesthetics' refers to a philosophical interest in the 'aesthetic experience of non-art objects and events'; and to a corresponding 'movement' in philosophical aesthetics, called 'Everyday Aesthetics', concerned with distinctions between 'fine and popular art' and 'art and craft'.[1] It could be reasonably added that the proper focus of philosophical interest in 'non-art' should be on design. And that as a movement the primary concern of everyday aesthetics should turn to the aims and work of designers. In other words, an everyday aesthetics worth the name is properly concerned with what I have identified as the 'design apology' and the philosophical concepts and issues that it raises.

Still, in turn, *its* issues, those of everyday aesthetics, are relevant to and feed back into design. So, I address some general philosophical issues in everyday aesthetics, examining how they relate to aesthetic functionalism about design. I argue that design is properly a core concern of the aesthetics of the everyday, both as subject matter and in contributing resolutions to its fundamental debates, especially about the nature and value of everyday aesthetic experience. So, in passing, I outline and examine a practical and theoretic tradition of everyday aesthetics available from William Morris, Walter Gropius, and designers with similar views, like Bruno Munari and Enzo Mari. In that context, of design's aims and work as 'everyday' and 'radically transforming', I examine the idea of 'world-making' in the Everyday

Aesthetics movement, as developed by Yuriko Saito in *Aesthetics of the Familiar*, and ideas of aesthetic education more generally.[2] I conclude that everyday aesthetics' activism is properly owed to the idea of good design.

Issues in everyday aesthetics

Texts in everyday aesthetics routinely cite John Dewey's *Art as Experience* (of 1934) as the starting point of the subject. But there is a history of the aesthetics of the everyday that precedes him and provides additional content and understanding to an aesthetics of the everyday. Indeed, there is a strong case that it has always been and will remain a fundamental concern, a philosophical inquiry into how we should live, with related moral, political, and ecological connotations. For example, Sartwell's double characterization of design needs reworking in the light of that as well as studies into design work. It is also worth noting here that everyday aesthetics has a central role in non-Western philosophy, one that also has a particular bearing on the philosophical aesthetics of design. I have already noted, constructing the design apology, the influence of Japanese 'Tea Philosophy' on Charlotte Perriand's design ideas, and the similar inspiration Kenya Hara has drawn and provides.[3] Such Daoist ideas on the nature of aesthetic experience and related notions of the possibilities for total experiential engagement with our everyday environment also have affinities with Deweyan ideas about heightened, valuable, and adaptive aesthetic experience beyond the confines of fine art. In any case, design's Western history predates Dewey, of course, and William Morris and the nineteenth-century Arts and Crafts movement, notably, clearly proposed an account that can reasonably be called an aesthetics of the everyday.

Indeed, Sartwell does state that 'the realm of the aesthetic' is established by acknowledging that 'there is an aesthetic dimension to a variety of experiences that are common to nearly all people, but would not normally be seen as experiences of fine art'.[4] He gives the supposed cross-cultural examples of 'body adornment' and the 'arrangement and ornamentation of [our] immediate environment in order to create a pleasing effect'.[5] Other examples are provided: the decoration of homes, gardening, and cooking; and popular music, web design, and film. Sartwell makes a further conclusion that the facts of everyday aesthetics demonstrate 'the continuity of the fine and popular arts, of art and craft, and of art and spirituality'.[6] Everyday aesthetics then is not concerned with making artworks but with the 'art of living'.[7] A number of notable, contentious issues for everyday aesthetics are raised by Sartwell's characterization.

In an overview such as Sartwell's we can forgive, but should still note, the limited range of examples from non-Western cultures. More problematically, the idea of the aesthetic seems narrowed in its phenomenology to a merely 'pleasing' experience. There is also an unjustified emphasis in thinking about the content of everyday aesthetic experiences on the popular arts rather than on quotidian things of use. These issues raise a general question then about what is being referred to by the 'art of living'? Similar issues are brought into focus by Barbara Jones's account of the 'unsophisticated arts'.[8] In short, an account of everyday aesthetics in terms of 'popular' arts and cultural activities risks bifurcating aesthetic experience both theoretically and practically around the supposed superiority of art appreciation and associated activities. Jones's characterization of the so-called popular arts does provide a useful contrast with the concerns of design, which in turn undermines any idea of an unsophisticated everyday aesthetics. So, Jones's 'unsophisticated arts are "the things that people make for themselves or that are manufactured in their taste"; and they are "harder, cruder, brighter, much less tasteful [than fine arts]"'.[9] They 'have certain constant characteristics. They are complex, unsubtle, often impermanent, they lean to disquiet, the baroque and sometimes terror'.[10] But what are these 'popular arts'? Is Jones revealing a previously hidden, yet familiar, area of aesthetic creativity and experience? But, unlike William Morris for example, Jones is not referring to things of everyday use and how they might be made well and enjoyed. Her examples range from taxidermy to fairground roundabouts, from tattooing to canal boat decoration. No mention of our lives with things and places of use. I note Jones's account because it shows in sharp relief how an idea of everyday aesthetics, though laudable in intent to reveal the range of aesthetic experience, can reduce to an aesthetics of the trivial, the inconsequential, an everyday aesthetics that is less about the fabric of lives than about how we escape its dreary everydayness.

It is a background problem that challenges even fuller, philosophically rigorous accounts of everyday aesthetics like Yuriko Saito's. In *Everyday Aesthetics*, she also takes as axiomatic that the range of objects of aesthetic experience is beyond art. Sartwell's idea of the 'art of living' might suggest that everyday aesthetics is an *extension* of art experiences to other objects. But Saito also challenges the nature of that experience itself, and the consequent 'special experienced-based aesthetics'.[11] She argues that everyday aesthetics, in addition to broadening the scope of things of aesthetic experience, represents a range of 'moments that do not especially stand out'.[12] So, many everyday *moments* thought outside the scope of aesthetics should be understood as aesthetic. Saito gives the example of something that is experienced as unpleasant, perhaps untidy, that generates an automatic aesthetic response that then prompts an action to tidy up. The fundamental idea of 'special' associated with aesthetic experience falsely neglects, for Saito, everyday mundane experience of the kind that, for example, prompts tidying.

A problematic defining stance of everyday aesthetics, prefigured I think in ideas about unsophisticated versus fine arts in Jones, is thus raised. That is the idea of a divided philosophical aesthetics based on two views of aesthetic experience, one of its everyday, prosaic character and the other as a response to works of art. This is clearly not in line with Sartwell's idea of a continuity running between aesthetically experiencing the everyday (albeit in his characterization) and artworks. Instead, everyday aesthetics is left to explain an apparent radical disjuncture in the idea of the aesthetic.

In defending that position, Sherri Irvin challenges not simply the range and focus on artworks of traditional Western aesthetics but ideas about aesthetic experience itself when she proposes that 'experiences of everyday life are replete with aesthetic character'.[13] Like Saito, Irvin rejects the idea that aesthetic experience is singularly 'special' across art and non-art activities in the way characterized by Deweyan accounts. Rather, 'everyday experiences are simple, lacking in unity or closure, and characterized by limited or fragmented awareness'; yet this 'does not disqualify them from aesthetic consideration'.[14] They are the experiences one has in the room one is in, right now, from the window perhaps, able to 'watch the ducks that are swimming around'; or go outside, walk down the dirt road 'and study the various colours of the dirt and the tyre tracks'.[15]

But the nature of design – especially in the light of Ludwig Wittgenstein's examples of the aesthetics of everyday life – suggests everyday actions to get things 'looking and feeling right' are basic to the aesthetic across the board and thus provide grounds for questioning Saito's and Irvin's divided aesthetics.

Two recent debates are illustrative of how aestheticians have engaged these fundamental questions related to the nature of aesthetic experience. One, between Irvin and David Davies, is illustrative of how broad agreement about the existence of aesthetic lives beyond appreciating artworks still leaves significant room for disagreement. In this case, dispute centres on what in fact makes an individual experience aesthetic and justifies the claims for the value of everyday aesthetic experience generally. A second debate, between Christopher Dowling and Kevin Melchionne, is similar in agreeing an everyday aesthetics, but disputing what makes an experience aesthetically valuable and whether art-like experience is still the paradigm case of aesthetic experience. In both debates, design is not considered. I refer to them though because at key points of difference in the arguments, an awareness and understanding of aesthetic functionalism about design would help resolution. I mark those junctures with a reference to the design apology.

Davies disputes Irvin's rejection of everyday aesthetics' Deweyan heritage.[16] Irvin rejects the Deweyan heritage that requires aesthetic experience to have 'unity' and 'closure'. And that this involves some active and critical encounter with the things being aesthetically appreciated. This puzzles Davies because he wonders how there can be any value in such personal verdicts, in the sensory pleasures described by Irvin. In turn, how then, without the cognitive and the evaluative elements of aesthetic experience, can Irvin's claims of the moral and environmental significance of everyday aesthetic experiences be justified? Davies looks to the philosophical aesthetics of Frank Sibley for support, but the argument is essentially that there is a necessary cognitive element in aesthetic experience or, in other words, a requirement that 'critical' reasons for liking are part of the experience. That is, an object of everyday interest must be sufficiently rich to warrant a description that enters a critical debate about aesthetic value. In fact, descriptions of the fit and contribution to feelings of harmonious living of using everyday things of use are integral to the design apology's aims, reflecting the depth of design. The cognitive character of aesthetic experience (everyday or art) is twofold: I describe it; you can then debate my evaluation. Irvin indeed removes this element of a Deweyan explanation of aesthetic experience. Davies concludes that Irvin's account leaves no way to distinguish aesthetic from non-aesthetic experience. But he still supports the idea of everyday aesthetics because with any evaluative model we can return to the everyday and still find everyday aesthetic experience worth the name. Indeed, the design apology suggests that we find it in good design.

Dowling, like Davies, is sceptical about the aesthetic credentials of uncritical, sensory, everyday experience.[17] Still, again like Davies, he supports the general thesis of everyday aesthetics that aesthetic experience goes beyond that of artworks. Responding, Melchionne offers a defence of Irvin's examples of her supposed everyday aesthetic experiences by suggesting that, even if personal, they represent a pattern of aesthetic living. Dowling then agrees that aesthetic experience extends beyond artworks, but its core is 'the normative aspect that renders certain judgements of particular interest to others'.[18] Aesthetic experience has an essential axiological dimension, in other words. So, 'there are good reasons not to overlook the distinction between merely idiosyncratic and a-critical responses and those that are putatively the subject of agreement, amendment, and critical discussion'.[19] Dowling's point is reasonable, but it does not exclude the experience of using everyday functional products. Trivial experience is non-social, non-critical: 'The kind of judgements that most of us are not required to engage with, falling to elicit the possibility of corrigibility, consensus, or criticism.'[20] Melchionne's response to Dowling argues for a view of everyday aesthetic experience where critical discourse is limited; and while conceding that individual experiences may not have aesthetic value in themselves, they represent aesthetic patterns of everyday life. That is, while the comfort of a breeze and so on in Irvin's account of her own aesthetic experience in her study might seem trivial, they are 'part of an extended ritual of study and reflection that the writer has honed' and show how 'ordinary experiences typically derive significance from their role in a pattern of daily life'.[21] It is perhaps moot whether this satisfies Davies's point that such experience can hardly support the greater claims of the Everyday Aesthetics movement. Certainly, if everyday aesthetic experience is not for its own sake but is also world-making (after Saito), then its critical and normative character would seem necessary. And this points to the significance of design as a creative, critical, world-making activity, as expressed in its design apology.

So, fundamental issues raised within everyday aesthetics about everyday experience and aesthetic value find resolution, I think, in the light of the design apology. Furthermore, when design's contribution to thinking about everyday aesthetics, predating the Everyday Aesthetics movement by one hundred years counting William Morris, is considered, there is more evidence of a non-trivial, deep, and extensive idea of everyday aesthetics.

Design and the idea of everyday aesthetics

I return to the most fundamental doubt about everyday aesthetics, namely its reality. So, while experiencing artworks is relatively rare, it might also be the case that aesthetic experience is not a quotidian feature of many lives, lives that are evidently and essentially non-aesthetic. Lives of poverty and squalor, for example, seem fundamentally so, without any possibility of some aesthetic compensation. The same could be said of lives dominated by over-consumption of poor quality and unnecessary things. But dissatisfaction with this miserable situation, with the state of the material world of things, is the general prompt for ideas about everyday aesthetics and good design from Morris at least in the era of mass production. Ideas about new products, homes, and cities are generated: about new ways of living. 'Art as life' mottos spring up. I note these thinkers about design not merely to make a historical point about the age and roots of everyday aesthetics but to reveal a fundamental philosophical difference. That is one between everyday aesthetics conceived as primarily about celebrating aesthetic experiences in the world as it is and a view, expressed by these thinkers, of its essentially transforming or revolutionary mode. Once more, Dewey's *Art as Experience* seems insightful and sets the tone.

Here, I simply note how Dewey relates his general theory of aesthetic experience to questions of design. There is no dedicated investigation of design's aims and work in *Art as Experience*. But Dewey does indicate that design has an experiential depth and a social extent that is significant in establishing a substantive (perhaps design-centred) everyday aesthetics. For example, the significance of design is evident in a statement about industrial design that 'aesthetic revolution [is] brought about by better adaptation to need.'[22] The idea of change is thematic in design work, of course, as designers reassess how needs are met by products and places as they are and could be to improve our experiential lives with them. In Deweyan terms, we experience things in use as adaptative in fitting ways that yield aesthetic results. Good design is part of that everyday integration of the human 'live creature' with her environment. In other words, designers contribute to the stock of aesthetic value in the world through good designs. Since aesthetic value, no less, is at stake, Dewey notes what he thinks are threats to 'art and civilization.'[23] Notably in terms of design, he sees it threatened by what he calls 'mechanical production', which he regards as anathema to aesthetic quality. And yet industrial conditions of production can still be manipulated to aesthetic ends by thinking about products' 'efficient use', for example by removing 'silly encumbering ornamentations.'[24] Dewey goes on to suggest that this 'revolution' extends from products themselves to how production – including of course design work, generally – is organized. So, he suggests that 'no permanent solution [to the absence of aesthetic quality in artefacts] is possible save in a radical social alteration, which effects the degree and kind of participation the worker has in the production and social disposition of the wares he produces.'[25] It is hard not to read into this statement the artistic and social ideals of William Morris and their relation to those of Walter Gropius, the founder of the Bauhaus.

In the same year, 1934, that Dewey is reflecting on design as experience, Walter Gropius reads a paper to the Design and Industries Association in the UK. The philosopher of art and design Herbert Read championed Gropius's 'ideals', 'which are not restricted to the written word, but which have been translated into action, made objective in the industrial world, and there demonstrated their truth and practicability'.[26] Read was writing in the context of the requirement, as he saw it in the light of Gropius, for a new industrial art for machine-made goods; for design in other words that was not a decorative or artistic add-on. So, Read quotes Gropius's paper at length. Of significance are Gropius's reflections on the work of the Bauhaus fifteen years after writing its Manifesto. So: 'Our object was ... to liberate the creative artist from his other-worldliness and reintegrate him into the workaday world of realities; and at the same time to broaden and humanise the rigid, almost exclusively material mind of the business man'.[27] And: 'Our guiding principle was that artistic design is neither an intellectual not a material affair, but simply an integral part of the very stuff of life.'[28] Finally, on its working methods: 'The Bauhaus ... workshops were really laboratories in which practical designs for present-day goods were conscientiously worked out as models for mass production, and were continually being improved on'.[29] It is little wonder that Read admitted to merely propagating these ideals of design creativity for improving everyday lives. They created then and still ground now the fundamentals of practical design – creative, iterative work designing goods for everyday use – and its larger social aims – an everyday, practical humanism through mass production of quality products used in our everyday lives.

The designer Bruno Munari also took inspiration from Bauhaus because its manifesto aimed to make a 'new kind of artist, an artist useful to society'.[30] Munari's loose use of the word 'art' is philosophically problematic for categorizing artistic work as essentially self-expressive and definably not about producing useful products. Still, the point is about designers' social role in making things that improve our everyday lives: so, 'when the objects we use every day and the surroundings we live in have become in themselves a work of art, then we shall be able to say that we have achieved a balanced life'.[31]

These revolutionary aims for design and by extension everyday aesthetics tend to utopianism in the design aims and design work of Enzo Mari.[32] He describes these aims in an interview as a 'lifelong project to transform the world through a socialization of design. By freeing us from simply being passive consumers of design he believed we could reorganize society according to core collectively conscious principles of material and intellectual production.'[33] What does this mean for design? Are there products that perform or help achieve personal transformation in our using them? Mari designed tables and chairs. So, for example, how does their design and use effect personal and social transformation? The questions are raised somewhat rhetorically. Still, there are philosophical answers to them. They are related to the role of the aesthetic in everyday life that Mari has evidently adopted from a Morrisian view of design, aesthetic lives, and society. Mari's interviewer concludes that 'his ideas for a new form of civilization were rooted in the cultural and social degradation that he saw around him, and that he fought against his entire life'. This statement about Mari rings entirely true of Morris.

Indeed, Morris's ideas about a design or 'art'-led everyday aesthetics reveal its problematic issues as well as its general aims. Two stand out. They are the efficacy of design work achieving transformative aims of human flourishing and to what extent these aims are 'political'; and about whether there is a 'style' that meets the requirements of personal and social transformation. Nikolaus Pevsner's historical account of modern design, published in 1936, culminates in the thoughts and work of Gropius but states Morris as its first pioneer, as having laid the foundations of the modern style in design thinking and work.[34] For Pevsner, Morris is a design pioneer because of the role he gives it in transforming lives. But he has problems squaring Morris's stylistic medievalism with modernism's look and feel.

So, it is worth attending to some theoretic disputes and misunderstandings about Morris's views on art and politics, especially as they pertain to design, before returning to Pevsner's account. Without engaging 'Morris studies', it is clearly wrong to separate 'art' and 'politics' in understanding Morris for the simple reason that his views on 'art' generated his political interests and provide their ultimate content. For example, it has recently been suggested that 'Morris became a socialist … because he thought everybody should be able to live in places like Red House'.[35] Red House is the home Morris designed with Philip Webb and a place he furnished to his own designs too. And one thing is certain: Morris signed his Socialist Federation membership card 'Designer'.[36] Owen Hatherley suggests that Morris 'needs to be seen both as designer and socialist at once'.[37] But what does this putative connection between design and socialism consist of? How does it unpack in theoretical terms? Hatherley's suggestion is a loose one about people living in pleasant places. So, for example, he links Red House's design to utopian housing schemes in early twentieth-century Britain, like the garden-city movement and local government social housing projects. Morris did indeed write on 'The Housing of the Poor', where his emphasis is on proper and beautiful dwellings for everyone. 'Housing the poor', for Morris, extended to the production of all things and was not a political goal *per se* but part of the wider ideal of living better, more aesthetic even, lives.

A couple of further things can be said with relative certainty about Morris's art and politics. One can be said quickly: it is not about *style* reflecting political ideas. Morris's own design work bears his creative mark, of course. But it is an artistic style, not a political one. Morris's concerns as a designer and maker are not set by any *a priori* political ideals but by aesthetic concepts like beauty and pleasure. The second certainty about Morris's art and politics is positive and substantive. He expresses it on numerous occasions. In short, it is that artistic ideals determine political goals. In 'How I Became a Socialist' Morris notes how 'politics as politics' never attracted him.[38] The ideal that drove Morris's commitment to socialist politics was 'the desire to produce beautiful things' and a 'hatred of modern civilization'.[39] Why the latter? Because, for Morris, its capitalist production, commercialism, and consumerism made it wholly inconsistent with the former, with producing beautiful things (with 'Art', for short, as Morris typically uses the word). The 'love of art' demands practical socialist politics to enact the economic and social conditions under which it flourishes. Still, why is art so important? Because, says Morris, 'it is the province of art to set the true ideal of a full and reasonable life'. Hatherley thus acknowledges Morris's art–politics nexus when suggesting that Morris presents 'a way of realizing what he imagined life would be like *as a designer*'.[40]

It is useful to briefly note a commentator on Morris who pursues this idea of the transforming role of design in human lives and the extent to which it is political, in the broadest sense of how we *ought* to live. Again, my focus on Morris's politics is meant only to indicate, albeit strongly, that a design-led everyday aesthetics necessarily embraces some political dimension. Florence Boos's 'Introduction' to his *Socialist Diary*, her *Socialist Aesthetics*, and her essay 'The Ideal of Everyday Life in William Morris's News from Nowhere', all link Morris's politics to his lifelong aesthetics.[41] She argues that Morris's conception of art precedes his politics; and that its conception depended on his concerns with the quality of things of everyday use, from chairs to places to live. She relates it back to his earliest, even childhood, thoughts about the beauty of cathedrals. Boos provides a theoretical framework to understand Morris's political writing, arguing that Morris extends art to (a) 'most purposeful and pleasurable activities' so that (b) it exposes the general 'exploitation of labour', and (c) its related 'organization of society for profit' so that (d) a claim is made for everyone to have 'a right to pleasure in labour'.[42] Morris's emphasis is on the design and production, rather than use, of things of everyday use. He is primarily interested in the pleasures of creative labour; his politics is motivated by that aesthetic aim. Still, it is significant that these pleasures are aesthetic and that they extend to our pleasures in using well-crafted things of everyday utility. In short, Morris's political ideals are aesthetic ideals. At the very end of his life Morris argued for socialism from core aesthetic and design principles rather than in the terminology of politics: 'for *use*, for *happiness*, for LIFE'.[43]

With this background understanding of Morris in mind, doubts that he founded the modern style are well-grounded. Morris's pioneering thoughts and work in relation to design are connected to modernist developments but in more complex and non-linear ways than Pevsner's account suggests. Gillian Naylor, for example, doubts Pevsner's thesis that Morris laid the foundations of the modern style, the style finally determined, at least in terms of modernism's 1930's high point, by Gropius.[44] I raise these points to indicate the fundamental difference between revolutionary thinking about design, its ideals, and the necessary iterative work of designing things and places to meet human needs, and the idea of a style that meets that overarching set of aims. There is a good case for arguing that Morris laid the foundations for thinking about design as necessarily about improving everyday lives. Also, that Gropius and the Bauhaus, and beyond, follow that fundamental idea. It warrants, too, an idea of everyday aesthetics that is design-led and revolutionary.

But Morris's essential radicalism about design was not prescriptive about style, except that a style should result in some pleasurable improvement in everyday living with things and be conducive to production under good working conditions. His radicalism resides in how what he termed a 'democracy of design' – all our homes filled with well-made and useful things – might also encourage a general change in the ways things of everyday use were made.[45] This was significant to Morris because he thought it would bring skilled making back into everyday working practices and lives. Gropius's 1919 Bauhaus Manifesto was illustrated by a woodcut of a Gothic cathedral, and it is supposed therefore that he alluded to Morris's idea that the various skills and workmanship, design, and planning, involved in building a cathedral, were exemplary of the integrated, broadly conceived artistic organization of good design work. For Morris, the Gothic cathedral demonstrated the 'freedom of hand and mind subordinated to the corporate harmony which made the freedom possible'.[46] By the 1930s, Gropius has moved to craftsmanship as part of the prototyping process of design within design studios. But Morris too had written on how a factory might be, admitting to some mass production for 'goods useful to the community'.[47] The key point is that their views on the organization of design work, on the relative roles of craftsmanship and mass production, on this or that stylistic look, were directed by design's aesthetic, transforming principles, rather than by any political imperatives.[48]

So, Morris and Gropius, and others thinking in their vein, are significant in developing an idea of everyday aesthetics grounded on the supposed developmental and transformative effects of good design. In that, they share a 'deep' experiential view of design's role in everyday life. That also establishes an idea of everyday aesthetics as properly engaged in aesthetic education and world-making. To reiterate, here I have examined these thinkers in terms of design and supposedly political aims, especially since their ideas resonate strongly with a renewed design 'activism' noted by Sudjic and, theoretically, with ideas about educating desires and world-making, the latter recently articulated by Yuriko Saito.

Aesthetic education and world-making

The idea of everyday aesthetics cast in the mould of thinking about design generates conclusions far removed from Sherri Irvin's about the educative and world-making possibilities of everyday aesthetic experiences. In the general spirit of everyday aesthetics Irvin states that aesthetic experiences 'should not be rare' and 'only accessible to art experts'.[49] But her examples of 'gardens in bloom' and the like are problematic for reasons of triviality and value. Irvin, as noted, effectively divides aesthetic appreciation between 'deep' and 'mere' and compromises the coherence and singular phenomenology of aesthetic experience as necessarily a confrontation with (dis)value. I examine these issues because they raise further problems for the ideas of aesthetic education and world-making that design-led 'activist' accounts of everyday aesthetics propose. It is thematic that design's work presents a depth of concerns, but Irvin's account of the 'merely everyday' results in her concluding two things that run counter to any notions of aesthetic education and world-making. They are: (a) that 'ordinary aesthetic appreciation' involves no necessary knowledge of what 'causes' one to enjoy something;[50] and (b) that developing a capacity for aesthetic experience is limited to a Buddhist-like one of self-training in 'mindfulness'.[51] While raising issues for Saito's world-making thesis, Irvin's neglect of the idea of aesthetic education is striking and requires addressing briefly first.

So, in summary, the philosophical idea of aesthetic education has traditionally been elaborated in two distinct ways: the 'art appreciative' and the 'moral-political'. Alongside these are various practical approaches to training artists, designers, and craftsmen, and to teaching the appreciation of artworks. The design apology appeals to the 'moral-political', not to the 'art appreciative' or practical, idea of aesthetic education. That is, it values design's ability to improve our everyday lives. I have witnessed that in the transforming or revolutionary design-led everyday aesthetics of Morris et al. Friedrich Schiller's *On the Aesthetic Education of Man* is the seminal work in the moral-political tradition. Paul Guyer places Schiller alongside William Morris, John Ruskin, and John Dewey in arguing that aesthetic experience allows a distinctive 'freedom to develop our imaginative and cognitive capacities, to gain knowledge of ourselves and others, and to imagine new ways of life, a freedom that is valued not simply for its own sake but also because of the benefits the developments of these capacities can bring to the rest of our lives'.[52] If this is indeed true of aesthetic experience, then in so far as good design delivers aesthetic experience, it is educative too.

This might seem a heavy burden for design to carry, even if only in part, but designers have an interest in the general social and improving effects of designs. Moreover, it does seem a defensible position that good design at least contributes to free and consensual societies by engaging with problems of human needs and cultivating sensibilities to them in making things and creating the built environment. Good designs evidence that we are capable of being free and proud shapers of our environments. This 'dignity of man' – the Renaissance idea of what humans can make and achieve *qua* humans – is perhaps the loftiest, humanist ideal of design and of making more generally. It is an ideal of making the best we can, which necessarily involves design work to create everyday things that allow human beings to flourish in making and using them.

It bears repeating that in design this is a common and garden ideal expressed through, for example, the overarching criterion of awards for good design. The UK 2017 Designs of the Year stated that 'Design can be defined as the improvement, or optimisation, of things.'[53] In that year, the improvement and optimization of things is elaborated in terms of the effects of design on 'production, distribution, use and waste' and more specifically design's environmental impact; also on how it can help 'access to information', and encourage 'cross-cultural communication'.[54] But whatever the details, designers continue to talk and write about the 'transformative power of design to change the way we live our everyday lives'.[55] For example, the transformative potential of good design to tackle ecological and social problems and having these as core non-commercial values was a determining factor in the 2019 RIBA prize-winning social housing estate.[56]

Explaining the transformative power of design has long been a concern for design educators. For example, William Richard Lethaby noted that while designers deal with 'very complex and technical matters' so that 'their works . . . show our science', their actual 'business is with civilization'.[57] Designers should be 'ministers of civilization', no less.[58] Lethaby thus saw the twofold character of design work and its education: 'train us [designers] to practical power, make us great builders and adventurous experimenters', but additionally '[design] education must be recast in the public service'.[59] Design work is considered to be about 'betterment all round' and work that is accordingly not at the mercy of commerce and patronage. But how is the idea that design work has an overarching 'civilizing' aim made clear to designers? Lethaby suggested that design students needed 'contact with larger ideas than "shop" and the passing of examinations'.[60]

Similar perspectives come from Saito's *Aesthetics of the Familiar*. The Everyday Aesthetics movement has always been developmental in its commitment to ideas about the extensive range of opportunities for aesthetic interest and experience and their value (as noted in introductory remarks to this chapter). But Saito's recent work now emphasizes areas of interest that mirror Lethaby's and the transforming view of everyday aesthetics of Morris, Gropius, and activist schools of design. So, in Saito's *Aesthetics of the Familiar* we see an aesthetics–society nexus suggested; the idea, that is, that our everyday aesthetic tastes and attitudes have serious, non-superficial consequences beyond the quality of our daily lives to the state of society and the world. Saito concludes that 'against the rather unfortunate, but prevalent, assessment of aesthetic matters as a dispensable, superficial icing on the cake, I argue that aesthetics is deeply entrenched in our daily lives, decisions and actions, all of which have serious consequences. Particularly today, aesthetics has become the prime mover behind capitalistic enterprises and a major factor in the political domain.'[61] Saito identifies three main areas in which everyday aesthetics has an impact: the sustainability of the world; relationships between people, with things, and with nature; the possibility of a 'humane and inclusive atmosphere'.[62] So, for Saito, living with everyday things takes on an 'ethical' dimension. An ethical dimension in choosing what to buy is evident in the way many products are marketed of course. And it is based on a familiar and basic, albeit true, understanding that what we buy determines what is produced and what is wasted, and on what kind of built environment we all live in. The role of everyday aesthetics, after Saito, is to draw attention to and educate our choices of products. Saito calls for ethically motivated aesthetic judgements; that more attention should be given, in considering 'our moral life', to how it is 'mediated by the aesthetics of objects we create or handle'.[63] So, a new normative discourse is required for everyday aesthetics; something more than a richer aesthetic phenomenology beyond the experience and appreciation of artworks. Why? Because of 'the power of everyday aesthetics to direct our actions'.[64]

Saito's laudable aims for everyday aesthetics are familiar ground for design work. But the design apology casts these so-called 'moral' aims in terms of good design, without recourse therefore to moral concepts or imperatives. At the cost of repetition, good designers deal in identifying real needs and in the contexts that Saito describes for a revitalized everyday aesthetics. So, for example, good designers think in terms of sustainability, functionality, and overall social effects. For Saito, this all amounts to a positive contribution to 'world-making'. This is surely correct. Still, for designers, it simply *is* their fundamental design apology. Indeed, it could be said that Saito is only expressing a version of it.

This is evident on some closer examination of Saito's analysis of the 'respect for humans expressed aesthetically through objects'.[65] Saito draws on examples from the 'Japanese artistic tradition' to support the idea of 'our moral life with things'.[66] The best example, she notes, is the tea ceremony – 'not the specifics of the host's aesthetic decisions, but rather the fact the host's concern for the feelings of guests is expressed through aesthetic means'.[67] Similarly, Japanese garden design reflects a 'desire to provide an optimal aesthetic experience to the visitors'.[68] But, in both cases, isn't a 'guest' or 'visitor' different to design's 'user'? As guests, Saito is right to suggest 'we participate … insofar as we recognize and respond to the aesthetic expression of care and respect'.[69] But, in that case we respond to the behaviour of the host, not the things as such. Saito additionally suggests that 'we tend to pass on kindness and consideration to those around us' in places expressive of care and thoughtfulness.[70] But, again, in such cases what and who are we responding to; and how? From these examples, Saito adduces positive and negative design practices. Positive designs 'continue the time-honored tradition of other-regarding consideration'.[71] But good design honours no traditions; and its regard for others is simply a necessary feature of designing things of general use. Saito quotes Kenya Hara's use in design work of the traditional Japanese artistic concept of 'emptiness' as supporting the fact that good designs are thus 'characterized by minimalism, simplicity, understatement, and the absence of showy self-assertion, while maintaining meticulous and thoughtful attention to detail'.[72] These are indeed attributes of good design in most cases. But only in so far as they accord with a solution to a design problem. We should agree with Saito that good design is not a 'mode of styling' or merely a 'branding' exercise.[73] But I have noted this as part of the general design apology, and it has roots within the development of professional design work. It can be explained as a focus on needs, function, and experience. Further moral and cultural explanations are unrequired, neither conceptually nor practically, for good design. However, that is *not* to say that exemplars of good designs and practices are not vital in aesthetic education; Saito's contribution in drawing attention to Japanese design and its philosophical traditions is important in that regard at least.

Still, Saito does concede that such concerns of good design in general are 'hardly unique to the Japanese tradition' and that 'care' is evident 'in the field of design today'.[74] We can agree – since they accord with the design apology – with Saito's list of positive aspects of the design process like 'courtesy', 'responsiveness', 'humility', and 'care'. Still, how they come into play depends on the nature of a design problem. Saito adds that products should 'honor the senses', but simply using a moral idiom does not alter the fact that doing so is essentially producing a good design. Saito is right to expand the idea of that success experientially to the 'senses'. But it is disputable, or a cultural idiom, to suggest that experiential success is moral, an 'honoring'. Certainly, in design work, as noted, ideas of 'honoring' the senses equate rather to notions of experiential fit and harmony. Saito's observations on buildings that 'make us feel at home' rightly direct us to that broader experiential and aesthetic sense of good design. But Saito insists on an explicitly moral view of the whole experience: 'the aesthetic value of designed objects . . . is not only in the enhancement of pleasure. It also communicates a moral attitude . . . by affirming the importance of others' experiences'.[75] I think, with the design apology in mind, this fails to recognize that good design work is essentially about care for 'others', in so far as designs are for general use. Saito is properly concerned by designs that only reflect the aesthetic sensibilities of the designer and not a design's users. But this is simply a case of bad design, not of bad morals.[76] It is telling that Saito's example comes from architecture, where one-off commissions for buildings invite starchitects and their aesthetic visions. But such work is outside of design and mass production.

Another example from Saito illustrates the point that good design does not require explicitly moral considerations in conceiving design problems and solutions. The example she uses is of the lack of signage at her local railway station (while Saito also acknowledges that too much signage and street furniture is a problem too). Saito rightly sees this as an essentially functional issue about user needs at a railway station. But, I think surprisingly, it is not then also identified as a standard *design problem* of identifying what people using the railway station need and creating a design solution offering the best experience for travellers. The railway station needs a designer to look into the problem, survey the station's users, consider the town's history and architecture, and so on. It is not an ethical issue. It raises no ethical dilemmas. It is not a problem solved by a moral attitude. The solution is well-designed signage.

The idea that this and related architectural examples indicate 'moral offences' is, I conclude, with the design apology in mind, wrong. Everyday aesthetics fulfils a vital service in identifying 'negative aesthetics' in the things we use and in our towns and cities. But I believe it is a mistake to conceive a fervent response to negative aesthetics as indicating a moral concern that, moreover, therefore requires a moral response of sorts. Ian Nairn is 'outraged' by the sights of Subtopia, much as Saito is by ugly public buildings, inconsiderately designed for the elderly for example, and poorly signed railway stations, and so forth. But it is not proper moral outrage and concern. 'Positive aesthetics' evokes high emotions too of course: Gropius lectured young architects on his ideas, and one, Maxwell Fry, reported that he 'filled us with a fervour as moral as it was aesthetic'.[77] That too is mistaken if, consequently, design problems are subjected to moral design principles, and solutions are deduced from them rather than from real, situated needs and functions.

Saito is right to suggest that the theoretic interests of everyday aesthetics – if it is serious about addressing questions about how everyday lives should be lived – should refocus on the things we design and use. It is right too to point out that non-Western traditions of 'care' about everyday things help direct that focus. The designer and potter Bernard Leach made this diary entry for 16 April 1952 after visiting the Tokyo industrial Art Institute: 'Came away feeling depressed by the chasm which separates the world of industrial design from the world of handcrafts . . . there was nothing in the buildings of their products which spoke to the heart through the senses.'[78] These are presumably sentiments, at least, Saito would applaud. Yet there is no moral imperative implied to design with 'care and concern'. What Leach thought was required was a 'modern craft movement' – like that in Scandinavia, he thought, then inspiring IKEA – an alliance, as he saw it, between industrial design and handcraft to create 'a new kind of designer'.[79] This designer would be knowledgeable about the world of machines and handcraft; and have 'an inside understanding of both Eastern and Western life'.[80] This marriage of ideas is more suggestive of the design apology's fullest expression than one urging a morally inspired everyday aesthetics and design.

We can also usefully follow Kenya Hara's thoughts on design as the 'education of desire', which are a continuation of Leach's, and ideas related to Japanese handcraft traditions. Hara's care is about the state of his nation, Japan. As a designer, he wants to be part of building a future for his country's people, working from its current, living circumstances and concerns but with traditions of good design in mind. But he recognizes that while good design aims to meet only real needs, the public might still hanker for and demand more of everything, with consumer demand easily triggered and manipulated by media and fashion. So, aesthetic education is required. 'If objects are created in response to human desires, the quality of those desires drives the quality of products and services, and of society itself'; so that 'our future happiness rests entirely on how we can educate our desires'.[81] Hara appeals, like Saito's attempts to cultivate aesthetic literacy and vigilance through everyday aesthetics, to the design apology's core concepts of needs and flourishing.

But it is not just about designing 'more stuff', therefore only compounding the problem of design characterized at the outset of this book. Hara contends that 'we should be prepared to throw things out'.[82] Aesthetic education in *that*, in knowing what is not needed, is as important to the overall aims of design expressed in the design apology as the positive contributions good design makes to world-making.

Conclusion

When design is properly included in the analysis of the idea of everyday aesthetics, there are two results: (a) everyday aesthetic experience is not understood as art's poor relation, neither theoretically nor practically; and (b) the concept of the aesthetic retains its integrity across art and non-art in terms of its experiential and cultural value. These are important contributions from analysis of design's work and aims – the design apology – to understanding aesthetic experience generally.

Moreover, aesthetic functionalism about design *ex hypothesi* supports everyday aesthetics' broad, educative, and developmental idea of the aesthetic in its iteration as a movement focused on everyday aesthetics as a world-making activity, as suggested by Saito. But aesthetic functionalism about design focuses that development on making and using everyday things well. Aesthetic education and world-making do not require the politicization of everyday aesthetics or moral guidance. Hara's thoughts on design and desire, for example, show that. In that vein, how designers make, and we use things well, is the topic of Part II.

Part Two

Design work

4

The personal experience of designed things

Introduction

A 2009 documentary film about design work, *Objectified*, has an opening scene which shows the production of designed things: simply, chairs being mass produced on a robotic assembly line.[1] Similarly, an introduction by Arthur Drexler to New York's Museum of Modern Art's (MOMA) design collection in 1973, now its Architecture and Design collection, characterized design as an activity 'concerned primarily with mass-produced useful objects made to serve a specific purpose'.[2] MOMA's collection, begun in 1932, was the first devoted to design; the first objects were 'culled from a "Machine Art" exhibition'.[3] Drexler, also the collection's curator, referred then to the 'arts of manufacture' and the categories remain familiar, from appliances and equipment to tableware and furniture. Reiterating what design is, he also refers to the variety of specific mass-produced artefacts from typewriters and radios to chairs, tables, and automobiles. The idea of 'machine art' or 'the arts of manufacture' was meant to convey the criteria for inclusion in the collection, namely artefacts that meet both functional and aesthetic conditions. In other words, these conditions were meant as the fundamental criteria of *good* design.

These two criteria are thematic in product design. But their character and relationship are less clearcut. Drexler refers to an object's aesthetic quality in terms of it being thought to achieve, or to have originated, those formal ideals of beauty which have become the major style concepts of his time. Styles do of course develop. But I argue that the development of styles is fundamentally connected to the need for products and so to problem-solving; not to adherence to 'ideals of beauty'. Anticipating that argument, it supports ideas that separate the aesthetics of successful products from what the American designer Raymond Loewy called disparagingly 'mere style jobs'. Drexler's second general criteria of good design related to functionality, however, does accord with aesthetic functionalism about design in so far as it reflects the character of ongoing product design and development, expressed as: 'Objects which may or may not resolve problems of aesthetics and function with total success, but which nevertheless have contributed importantly – or may yet contribute – to the development of design.'[4] In examining the need for products, product designers' views on their work, and examples of how needs and products change, the richness and complexity of the functionality and aesthetic experience of everyday things emerges, challenging engineering or austerely functional views of good design work.

The need for products

The idea that design work is essentially a practical problem-solving activity directly related to human needs was stated by the American designer Henry Dreyfuss as an anthropological intuition about the very beginnings of design: 'primitive man, desiring water, instinctively dipped his cupped hands into a pool and drank. Some of the water leaked through his fingers. In time he fashioned a bowl . . .; attached a handle . . .; pinched the rim to make a spout', thus following the same principles of need and utility that guided Dreyfuss's industrial design company creating products for mass production.[5] Anthropological studies provide supporting evidence. In understanding the earliest use of stone implements, 'the hominid ancestors of modern people . . .

invented a tool type, with specific purposes in mind, which they went on to make and make again'.[6] The simplest choppers functioned to cut meat, bones, roots, and bark. But it is generally assessed that as these tools developed, they had soon 'aesthetic qualities that went beyond functional needs': 'the human interest in the artefact – the crafted object, both as useful item and a bearer of some kind of style – was born'.[7] In a similar vein, the curator of the British Museum invited the naturalist Sir David Attenborough to hold and comment on its oldest artefact, an Olduvai stone chopping tool made two million years ago. He speculated that the maker must have got 'some satisfaction from knowing he was doing it very effectively, very economically and very neatly... in time, you would say he'd done it beautifully'.[8] This characterization of 'aesthetic' in relation to made things emphasizes felt experience in making, and by extension in use, rather than any conscious stylistic imperative.

Plato's philosophical analysis of the beauty of implements is similarly grounded in need, function, and use. So, he argues:

> do not the excellence, the beauty, the rightness of every implement, living thing, and action refer solely to the use for which each is made or by nature adapted? That is so. It quite necessarily follows, then that the user of anything is the one who knows most of it by experience, and that he reports to the maker the good or bad effects in use of the thing he uses.[9]

Plato effectively argues then for the primacy of direct, unmediated user experience in determining the value of implements. Designers refer to users' experience in arriving at good designs. The very earliest artefacts engage making and using in one person. But, a fundamental designer/maker-user dialectic is there, until it becomes a relationship, as it remains now, between separate but engaged designers and users of products. From anthropological evidence and Plato's fundamental understanding of implements, we see the practical and theoretic components of the protean character of design. Design work is ever-changing with successful adaptations, marked by aesthetic experiences of fit, that are then assessed anew by both makers and users of things as human needs alter. This adaptive work remains, sometimes more sophisticated, sometimes still about the experience of grip, for example, in designing kitchen products.[10]

Such an experiential understanding of the development of designs is argued by Gottfried Semper's analysis of style and is taken up by Adolf Loos's idea that 'ornament is crime'. Their broadly shared view is important to note because, in short, they relate the idea of beauty to practical success, to meeting needs. They do so in a way that supports explanations of aesthetic interest in good designs in practical, experiential terms, rather than in terms of the formal aesthetic properties of products. A product might, for example, be formally described in terms of its elegance and colour; but that would say nothing about its usefulness. Loos makes the point that a beautiful *product*, like a chair, is necessarily functional.[11] Functionality is not a sufficient condition for aesthetic value though. From understanding the design apology, aesthetic experience in using the product, our felt experience of fit and harmony, determines that value.

Gottfried Semper addresses the art of ceramics noting that 'the earliest and most general application of this art was without doubt to satisfy needs: eating, drinking, and washing above all'.[12] Furthermore, he notes, for example, how different uses in 'scooping' water from a river and 'catching' water from a fountain relate to the different forms of the ancient Egyptian situla and the Greek hydria (Fig. 2).[13] Loos quotes Semper in support of his view that the practical does not exclude the beautiful: 'show me the pots that a civilization has produced and you can generally tell what it was like'.[14] Loos adds that 'any utilitarian object can tell us of the customs, the character of a people'.[15] Scooping versus catching determines the form of these vessels. The

Greek hydria – a pot for fetching water – is formed as it is because of several practical factors: how the pots were carried by Hellenic women; how the pots were lifted, carried, and gripped. Loos argues for the idealistic view that such vessels reflected only an urge to beauty when in fact the form, the foot, body, handle, and size of mouth of the hydria, are determined by use.[16] He states: 'I would like to suggest that the ancient Greeks . . . know something about beauty. And [yet] they only worked practically, without even thinking for a moment about beauty, without trying to pursue an aesthetic need.'[17] Loos concludes that 'beauty' – in such instances – is an aesthetic concept applied to something that could not be made more practical. So, in Semper's and

Figure 2 Greek hydria, 7th–3rd century BCE. Gibon Art / Alamy Stock Photo.

Loos's accounts the aesthetic value or beauty of a useful product supervenes on its practical success. But while this might account for ascriptions of 'beauty' to practical things in terms of their formal appearance, still for design work the essential aesthetic character of good design is attested through aesthetic experience in use.

Certainly though, Semper's and Loos's analysis accords with, for example, the Eameses' design apology, and the apology more generally, in terms of design's concern with 'style'. The Eameses 'saw design not as the pursuit of originality for its own sake, but as a process of thinking about problems and their connection to surrounding historical, social and technological conditions'.[18] In other words, problem-solving defined their approach: their 'conception of design' was not defined by specific products they designed but rather by that outlook.[19] Generalizable across good design and integral to the design apology, rather than an Eameses' 'look', the Eameses aimed at something they called 'way-it-should-be-ness'.[20] This is surely just another way of phrasing anthropological insights about the aesthetics of early human tools and those insights of Plato, Semper, and Loos on the needs-based and experiential grounds of good design.

Loos, notoriously, chose a motto connecting 'ornament' with 'crime'. Reflecting on the paper 'Ornament and Crime', Loos later qualifies it or at least counters any crudely puritanical interpretation and action. He does state that 'Modern people, people with modern nerves, do not need ornament. On the contrary, they abhor it. All objects we call modern are without ornament. Since the French Revolution, our clothes, our machines, our leather goods, and all objects of everyday use have been without ornament.'[21] But asked 'are there cases where ornamentation is needed (for practical, aesthetic, or educational purposes?)', he replies:

> I maintained that the use of ornamentation on objects of practical use would disappear with the development of mankind . . . by that I did not mean what some purists have carried *ad absurdum*, namely

> that ornament should be systematically and consistently eliminated. What I did mean was that where it had disappeared as a necessary consequence of human development, it could not be restored.[22]

If these statements are set in the context of the design apology, they become more reasonable and do not allow a philistine or anti-aesthetic interpretation of 'ornament is crime'.[23] Especially since Loos relates the 'crime' of 'ornamentation', in one aspect, to a 'waste of good material' rather than some stylistic aesthetic.[24] That, at least, accords with the general problem of design, set out at the outset, of producing too much of poor quality at a cost to our experiential lives and the environment. Also, Loos is clearly describing the kind of design solutions expected of design problems for mass-produced items of everyday, functional use. Loos is interested in modern civilization. He understands design's key role in defining any civilization and that in Semper's practical terms about satisfying needs. And so, perhaps like Hara's concern to 'educate desires' for products, Loos argues against ornament on educative aesthetic grounds, that good design principles might influence our needs, allowing design to improve the world and build a sustainable, civilized future. Aesthetic education is necessary to counter a 'collective will of mankind which compels the producer to create those forms demanded by the cultural community as a whole'.[25] In that spirit, Loos accepts design ornamentation 'that brings order into our lives', where ornamentation works like grammar does in learning a language, giving us a shared, common fund of forms and aesthetic concepts.[26] But, to reiterate, this is a notion of 'ornamentation' as perfection, a product that requires no more or less about it.

In terms of the design apology, good design educates the need for products by, in its turn, meeting needs simply and effectively. So, the test of good design is always experiential. These general ideas of educative and iterative needs-meeting resonate throughout good design work. They are evident in, for example, Bertram's interwar modernism and in the 1951 South Bank Exhibition in the UK; but both cases run deeper than a modernist style or the stock list products compiled by a National Council of Industrial Design. Bertram made 'a general appeal for plain unornamented furniture. This is not because ornament is always bad.'[27] He acknowledges that in pre-industrial times, ornament of everyday functional items was often good but that it was so because 'it grew out of the intimate relationship between a craftsman, his materials and his tools'; and the ornament was 'integral with the object'.[28] That is, pieces of a chair, its legs, arms, panels, for example, were carved. Whereas modern ornament on mass-produced items is stuck on after the piece of furniture is produced, merely 'beautifying' – meant in a strongly pejorative sense – it.[29] The problems of design conceived as an artistic add-on or as absurdly irrelevant to the function of the product – problems noted by Dresser and Loos among others – were still being addressed then by designers, like Bertram, long after the 1851 Great Exhibition. But Bertram, like Loos, perhaps acknowledges that for millennia, design solutions were delivered by what we can roughly, but reasonably, call craft-like planning and delivery, where ornamentation was an integral part of the production process. Conceiving design problems and solutions for mass production using machinery marks the point at which design work is associated with professional designers, and their work becomes established as industrial design with its own principles, professional qualifications, and standards. And the general progression of industrial design seems to indicate an increasing range and depth of the idea of 'need' and therefore of 'function' in conceiving design problems and solutions. At the time design was establishing itself as a profession, Bertram produced a guide *Design in Everyday Things* for the general public showing its range of interests.[30] The guide accompanied a series of weekly, educative radio broadcasts. The range he indicated is now familiar, from furnishing and equipment of the house, through housing, transport, roads, shops, clothes, town and country planning, public buildings, to more specific things, like typewriters and stamps and fountain pens, reflecting the state of 1930s technology. The apogee in this UK tradition of educative, aesthetic, and functional design was perhaps the 1951 UK South Bank Exhibition's use of a 'Stock List', compiled by the UK's National Council of Industrial Design, which provided a standard for everyday products centred on their 'workmanship', 'appearance', and 'fitness for purpose'.[31] In the United States the equivalent of a quality mark was 'Good Design': the 1950 'Good Design: An Exhibition of Home Furnishings' showcased products that met a set of criteria that were also labelled with a 'Good Design' logo and sold across the country.[32] Still, the general spirit in which the need for products is cast remains. So, more recently, for example, the humble light bulb can be redesigned and win a design award as 'a masterclass in using imaginative design to transform something of bland utility into a thing of coveted beauty, which then becomes more usable and more enjoyable'.[33]

In summary, the general everyday need for products of high quality is recognized by governments through standards and design awards. It is a fact that museums, as well as retailers, are now dedicated to showcasing good design: examples are London's Design Museum and the Vitra Museum in Germany. Both museums grew out of design entrepreneurship and witness the close connections between design, aesthetics, and mass production of everyday goods.[34] In all that, it is clear that good design is driven by more than mere functionalism about meeting the need for products.

Product designers

When Raymond Loewy arrived in America from France in 1919, he was struck by the contrast between 'the excellent quality' of production and its 'gross appearance, clumsiness, bulk, and noise'.[35] It is a seemingly contradictory statement if 'quality' necessarily disengages the attributes Loewy lists. In fact, it reflects a classic but false – given aesthetic functionalism about design – division in design thinking between aesthetics and engineering. Yet Loewy is properly alluding to that and to his aim as a designer to 'combine an aesthetic sensibility with my professional background in engineering'.[36] In that combination Loewy thereby saw himself as a pioneer introducing the 'concept of industrial design'.[37] The introduction of aesthetics to engineering introduces real user needs to the concept of design and is integral to the design apology. An interviewer notes that Loewy's remodelling work on products involved improvements in visual appearance of a product that in fact were 'a functional step forward'; to which Loewy replied 'that's right. And that is the nature of industrial design.'[38] By the time Loewy and industrial design were established in the United States, a MOMA press release indicated key features of the work of product designers and links between engineering, technology, mass production, and showcasing end products.

> The exhibition, however, is not entirely confined to chairs. Additional strong, light pieces for dining room, living room and outdoors are included. New principles of construction in furniture are incorporated as a result of new techniques developed for mass production. The furniture is not currently available, these being merely the first models, developed and made under mass-production conditions by the Evans Products Company of Detroit, which is arranging for large-scale production.[39]

The air of easy-going confidence in design work in that press release is in marked contrast to the current concerns of the design profession. An editorial for an issue of *Disegno* in 2022 speculates on the fate of the young designer now. She probably 'dreamt of working within social design or crafting affordable products and housing solutions that could make an impact around the world'.[40] Of implementing the design apology in its fullest extent, it could be said. But the editorial continues 'yet good intentions quickly fade when faced by economic realities'.[41] Dieter Rams expressed a version of this situation, using the term 'counterpoints' to describe the situation from the 1970s that has required designers to posit alternatives to tackle the 'contradiction between the logic of the market and human ends'.[42] My focus here is on 'human ends' and 'impactful' design and what that means for product designers in terms of aesthetic functionalism about design.

The designer James Irvine, interviewed in 2003, thought designers 'spend time designing things which don't solve any problems, like designing another chair, or something like that, rather than confronting real problems'.[43] He later redesigned the Thonet Side Chair No.14, originally designed in the 1850s, for MUJI, to attract a young demographic to buy it (Fig. 3).[44] Still, in 2003 the design apology has some force in Irvine's mind: 'I try to design things that are true to themselves and not too influenced by marketing factors, things are for people, because my clients are people, not industry.'[45] And:

> some people think that design is a sort of styling thing, but I don't see it like that. I think it is cutting away all the bullshit and starting from the basics. It is one of the oldest tricks in the book, it is starting from scratch, starting from what I know and how I feel it should be and doing the object how I would do it. It has nothing to do with minimalism, more to do with cutting away to find the true strengths of my idea.[46]

These latter thoughts betray an egoism about design that Irvine also later contradicted. Introducing a monograph of his designs, its editor notes that while Irvine was in Japan – the Japanese design influence again is evident – he wrote that 'often designers change things for change's sake when the product has spent decades being gently nurtured to maturity. There is no need to destroy this functional and cultural presence.'[47] Still, 'there must be no fear of laying our hands on it and reassessing its expression'.[48] Irvine admits these seemingly contradictory factors in design work as the 'Design Dance' and relatedly as the 'Utopian Design Antibody'.[49] Both are pictures, part pictogram, part words, by Irvine: the former illustrates a designer forced to 'dance' to the competing demands set by form, function, people, and industry; and around those cluster more particular, seemingly conflicting, demands about technology, jobs, ecology, wealth...; the latter picture of an 'antibody' similarly sets design's utopian aspirations – the kind expressed in the design apology – against egotism, greed, waste, materialism, vulgarity, hegemony, and banality. His pictures represent, perhaps, more than Irvine's mental state *qua* designer. Perhaps, in short, they represent the real competing demands of design work, and in the theoretic terms set out here, represent the general problem of design confronting the design apology. An answer to the competing demands put on product designers like Irvine might be that suggested by Lou Downe, that 'good designers are half pragmatic and half idealistic' so that primarily a designer has 'to be willing to put someone else's needs over [their] own ideas'.[50] Downe understands this compromise in terms of the designer as primarily asserting their 'artistic' ego, suggesting that products need foremost to work well, and the designer's role is not about making something look better. Downe invokes the idea of functionality and aesthetics as 'the same thing' and the modernist dictum that 'form follows function'.[51]

There is evidently still confusion, within the profession, about what a product designer properly does. How competing demands on design work are met to produce good design. The idea of the *named* designer as essentially an artist or arbiter of good taste is alternatively raised and rejected in reflections on design work and its aims more generally. Some design history clears the ground for a theoretic resolution of the so-called artistry of design work by individual product designers.

Christopher Dresser was familiar with Semper's ideas about style and its relation to functional, design problems, having attended Semper's lectures at the UK's Government School for Design in the

Figure 3 Thonet Side Chair No.14, 1859. Gibon Art / Alamy Stock Photo.

early 1850s.[52] At the same time, a 16-year-old William Morris was reacting to the industrial art on show at the 1851 Great Exhibition in London by refusing to join a family visit. Whether teenage rebellion or an early indication of his design apology, Morris's view in fact chimed with Dresser's and others that many of the British products of everyday use failed on Semper's principles. So, Dresser noted the absurdity of designs like 'candle-sticks formed as human beings, with a candle fitting into the top of a chimney-pot hat or into the head; egg-cups formed as birds' nests'.[53] The same age as Morris, this recollection of the products of the Great Exhibition subsequently squared with his experiences of Japanese design of everyday things after a visit in 1877. The influence of that visit is a matter for biography and critical appraisal of his work. But it is worth quoting Dresser's acknowledgement of his debt to Japanese design principles evidenced, for example, in his electroplated teapots: 'A simplicity of treatment, and a boldness of design, which, when mingled with a perfect understanding of the method by which the design has been produced, stamp them as of great excellence' (Fig. 4).[54] Here I note two things of interest for aesthetic functionalism about design: (a) design is not conceived as applying 'artistic' work to a functional item; the good designer is knowledgeable about materials and making generally, including industrial production processes; but (b) Dresser does apply his signature to mass-produced products he designs.[55]

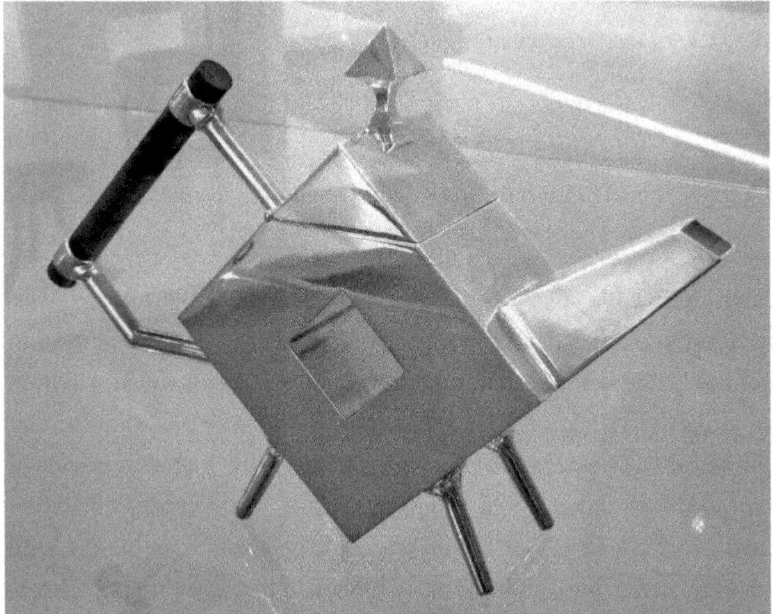

Figure 4 Christopher Dresser teapot, 1879. Reproduced under a Creative Commons Attribution-Share Alike 3.0 Unported license via Wikimedia Commons.

How is this resolved in thinking, in terms of the design apology, about designers as essentially 'needs-meeters'? Critical thinking about the issue suggests that design's 'artistry' *qua* 'creativity' is not intrinsic to design work or at best has a meaning that is unique in the context of design. So, Kees Dorst associates a certain kind of design creativity with artistry, arguing that where designers develop their own goals, and build these into projects, they 'are something of artists'.[56] He thus suggests that design's supposed art status resides in the 'artfulness' of self-generated goals, rather than in some shared, transferable practical skills or professional standards between designers and artists. For Dorst the point at which designers are artists is that at which they develop an individual 'style', albeit one that is only enacted through the possibilities for creativity set by design problems. But this means there is a key difference with art too: while a designer's goals are essentially set by others, because stakeholders in the product require a practical need to be met, artists set their own goals. Norman Potter similarly argues that the key difference between art and design work is in the 'freedom' artists have to generate works. He notes that a designer's outputs, like models and drawings, are neither ends in themselves nor are they the sole output of the designer's vision but rather the outcome of many discussions with clients and other stakeholders. These might be procedures familiar to artists – especially artists working on public or other commissions of course – but still the origins of artistic work are more inward, so that 'a painter's first responsibility [unlike a designer's] is to the truth of his own vision'.[57] Again in a similar vein to Dorst, Potter characterizes design's 'artistry' in a 'shared visual sensibility' or a designer having a sense of 'style'.[58] But that does not direct us to any necessarily common skills, procedures, or general aims for art and design. Creativity in design may be evidenced by 'style', but that is not evidence of 'art'. It marks imaginative, practical problem-solving.

Some designers themselves perhaps baulk at this non-artistic analysis of their work. There is some false encouragement for them too when designs are described as masterpieces and gifted descriptions more suitable for artworks. For example, Philippe Starck's Juicy Salif lemon squeezer is categorized, along with other 'great designs', in terms of style and structure as well as its 'expressiveness', and Starck's oblique quote supports this: 'When I design, I don't consider the technical or commercial parameters so much as the desire for a dream that humans have attempted to project onto an object' (Fig. 5).[59]

Figure 5 Philippe Starck Juicy Salif Citrus Squeezer, 1990. Chris Willson / Alamy Stock Photo.

Deyan Sudjic, in contrast, suggests that the named artist-designer, rather than the design team, is a 'fairy tale', laying that blame to start on Raymond Loewy, because he 'helped to turn design into a fairy-tale narrative free of complexities or subtleties'.[60] He is accused of the very thing Loewy stated was not design proper, merely giving engineered products like the Gestetner duplicator a new skin or look. Sudjic argues that examining products in terms of what they deliver, we get to 'what really drives design'.[61] When he refers to designs that do not respond to needs but involve 'arbitrary shape-making', lemon squeezers that do not catch the pips come to mind.[62]

Sudjic's reminder of anonymous design – the kind of design that produced zips, paper clips, and safety pins – usefully returns thinking about product designers to the fundamental issue of the need for products and how that is best met.[63] Highlighting that good design is not delivered by the 'obtrusive signature', 'egotism', and 'the cult of individual genius' is one way of doing that.[64] But what then of aesthetic functionalism about design? The designer Eddie Opara offers a rhetorical question that is a reasonable and due warning against puritanical functionalism. Product designers are more than problem solvers, he contends, because they never actually 'solve': 'take an example of a chair. When was a chair solved?'[65] Aesthetic functionalism about design does not imply the need for artists. Still, I think an appeal is made to an aesthetic and experiential rather than engineering notion of 'solved'.

Chairs and other things

Deyan Sudjic writes that 'few objects have attracted so much attention from so many designers as the chair'.[66] He thinks it is hard to say why there have been so many attempts to make new solutions to a problem that's been solved so often. Similarly, he had previously written that 'it would be possible to trace the history of design in the past 150 years simply through a sequence of chairs'.[67] So, why do designers keep (re)designing chairs? In the 1850s, the furniture manufacturer Thonet developed a chair, Side Chair No.14, for mass production that is now reasonably claimed to be 'probably one of the most recognizable, most produced, and most reinterpreted chairs of all time'.[68] Le Corbusier enthused that 'Never was a better and more elegant design and a more precisely crafted and practical item created.'[69] So, had the straightforward design problem set by him – that 'Chairs are made to sit in' – been solved once and for all?[70]

Sudjic's answer is that chairs have a variety of 'purposes that go far beyond utility' that give them 'cultural significance' related to 'power and status'.[71] So, 'the chair as a category will still be relevant even into the distant future' because 'the act of sitting is unlikely to go the same way as listening to vinyl records, or buying newsprint'.[72] The argument and contrast are poorly conceived. Sudjic's non-chair, counterexamples are of *redundant technology* within categories of products that are perhaps as timeless as the chair's need, namely 'listening to recorded music' and 'getting information from news media'. Still, if chairs for sitting will always be needed, is it because of the non-utilitarian purposes they meet? Loos, for example, suggested otherwise and more narrowly functionally in stating that chairs change over time as postures related to resting change. He cites the 'English and Americans ... [as] genuine virtuosi in the art of resting'; to the extent that 'according to the principle that every kind of fatigue calls for a different armchair, the English room never shows an entirely identical type of armchair. All kinds of seating opportunities are represented in the same room'.[73] It perhaps echoes this remembrance of William Morris's reaction to a poorly designed sofa: '"Sofa!" cried Morris "call *that* a sofa! It's a perch ..."'; a remark that illustrates a designer's concern with how we sit well in different types of chairs for different purposes.[74]

Sudjic goes beyond that level of aesthetic, directly experiential utility, giving an example of how the Eames Lounge Chair was designed with a particular kind of cultural experience and felt pleasure in mind: Eames

> wanted to create a chair that spoke of the creased, well-worn ease of a patrician East Coast club chair, with the lived-in appeal of a used soft leather baseball glove. Its buttoned leather upholstery shows off the tactile qualities of a material that ages with grace. Its cushions . . . allowed for a pleasing degree of wear with time as they took on the imprint of those who sat on them.[75]

No doubt similar intentions lie behind the designs of everyday things of utility that are used in ritualized settings, like taking tea, or are meant for use on special occasions. Glenn Parsons account of design includes the claim that chairs can never have 'expressive power or meaning'.[76] For Parsons chairs can be symbolic, expressive of a zeitgeist. But Sudjic's example of the Eames Lounge Chair suggests that designers can at least include in their conception of a design problem for a chair an intended experience of sitting that is richer than comfort, one that is an experience of a cultural ambience.

Chairs also change for more prosaic reasons of new material or technological opportunities to meet needs in better ways. Using Charles Eames again, this 1946 MOMA press release sums it up:

> The chair is king in the exhibition New Furniture Designed by Charles Eames opening at the Museum of Modern Art Wednesday, March 13. But not the ordinary chair. The exhibition will present the greatest innovation in chair design since Marcel Breuer startled the furniture world with his metal chair and Alvar Aalto introduced the technique of laminated wood furniture. Basically, the new Eames chair is a development for mass production of the molded-chair idea invented by Eames and Saarlnen, which won first prize in the Museum's Organic Design Competition in 1940–41. But

> something has been added – in fact, several things. Although the chairs still employ the molded back and seat construction sculptured to fit body contours, many new techniques and esthetic innovations are presented.[77]

Here is a more recent example, a twenty-first-century modernist chair, a single-piece, cantilevered lounge chair, previously technically unachievable. The designer is Jasper Morrison who explains: 'what we've done is take the very simple basis of an idea and execute it as purely as possible. It's a celebration of the technology of plywood.'[78] A critical evaluation is the 'result is both elegant and restrained, comfortable and technically advanced, all at the same time.'[79] Here are the experiential and functional criteria, at least, of good design for products in a nutshell: an integrated experience of visual appeal and physical comfort in use; and the best it can be technically.

So, in summary, why keep designing chairs? There are three fundamental reasons – that is, that apply to all designed products to lesser and greater degrees:

1. The needs associated with the basic functional requirements of sitting (or whatever basic need and function are being addressed) are various depending on activities associated with it and these change over time.
2. There is a creative appeal for designers, the challenge of meeting needs in new ways which will also create a signature of their work.
3. Materials and technologies change allowing design problems to be re-examined and new design solutions created.

Furthermore, our needs are met experientially. Designers solve design problems product by product, but our experiential lives are not solved but exercised. Our notions of fit and harmony with designed things change too. Take the example of designing a TV. What considerations of aesthetically experiencing the physical apparatus apply? Surely it is simply a design problem set by technological and commercial concerns to make TVs thinner and thinner. But some TV designers now wonder about the role the TV plays for some people in their lives apart from watching TV programmes. Such designers note the drive to simplify TVs to the point that they have no qualities apart from those determined by technology making screens ever thinner. But what if the TV is effectively a friend in the home for an isolated individual? Meeting that need might mean reconceiving the design problem for at least some TVs so that they function as an object that is part of a home too, with its associations of warmth and comfort, rather than just offering an experience of technological chic. What kind of TV, design solution, is required in such a case?

If this is true of TVs – that needs associated with a single functional type can be various across different users – then it is surely true of other products, even ones where technology seems the be-all and end-all. General analyses of the aesthetic experiences of specific products are thus thrown into doubt too. So, for example, Janet McCracken offers an analysis of why we like and use our mobile phones.[80] She argues that despite claims about psychological dependence on mobile phones for practical life, we love our phones for the same reason we love most things: for their beauty and for our possession of them. But no mobile phone designer could effectively work with this view, which offers nothing of our various uses of it and its many experiential roles. Acknowledging a debt to Rams's design principles and designs like the 1958 T3 pocket radio, Jonathan Ives's iPhone, for example, focused on users' needs rather than, in McCracken's terms, the 'gadget' itself.

In the 1950s Henry Dreyfuss found a constant reminder of the essence of design work in 'Joe and Josephine', line drawings of a man and woman placed on the walls of his design offices: 'They remind us [designers] that everything we design is used by people, and that people come in many sizes and have varying physical attributes.'[81]

Dreyfuss also lists a variety of tasks performed by 'Joe and Josephine' in their everyday lives. And he identifies one task for designers: 'Our job is to make Joe and Josephine compatible with their environment.'[82] It is one task with infinite variety. A glance at the range of designs nominated for the UK's Designs of the Year in 2019 and 2020 testify to that. This sample shows that range but also the specificity of designs in the twenty-first century: a toy block to teach Braille; a privacy-protecting set of spectacles; a carbon-conscious credit card; a plaster for every skin tone; a multifunctional bike accessory; a handle that disinfects itself; a homeware collection made from rice residue; a plastic-free edible drinks capsule; a stool with a useful shelf; a mobility robot; a speaker system with personality; a post-disaster water filter; a rug for a post-Snapchat world; an add-on to make crutches more comfortable; and, notably, a chair made of waste that will last for life.[83]

So, our experiential lives now demand more from designers than Dreyfuss could conceive via researching 'Joe's and Josephine's' lives. But however increasingly diversly and richly we conceive humanity, 'Joe and Josephine' still represent a core idea that good designers design products *for people* to use in ways that engage and enhance *their* experiential lives.

Conclusion

Understanding the need for products, the why answered anthropologically and then in terms of the variety of human needs, plus that evidenced in product designers' ambitions and work, supports aesthetic functionalism about products. It, in turn, suggests the arts and crafts motto that, in the case of products, 'beauty takes care of itself'.[84] It does so in these two ways: (a) the aesthetic value of products is marked in our useful and pleasurable use of them in our everyday lives; and (b) good designers respond to the evolution of needs met aesthetically by products in use not merely in form. In that, the depth of aesthetic experience – its distinctive phenomenology and relation to value – available to good design is the same as that available to art. But no doubt designers clinch it on different – functional – occasions than artists. This chapter has looked at one set of occasions, products. Chapter 5 looks at another, namely homes.

5

The beauty of life: design and everyday living

Introduction

Design has a concern with that band of aesthetic interest at the everyday, household level that lies between the design and appreciation of individual products and that of the built environment.[1] Its aesthetic interest in domestic interiors can be dated to the impact of the Aesthetic Movement on mass design at the end of the nineteenth century. Charles Eastlake's *Hints on Household Taste* was published in 1878, concerned with the need for 'improved taste in objects of modern manufacture' that make up the 'internal fittings of a house'.[2] He advocated 'simplicity of style'.[3] Eastlake's 'hints' were aimed at both consumers in their choices and at designers, proposing principles of good design for industrial art, for designing 'artistically appointed houses'.[4] He challenged both any supposed 'indifference to art' by the public and any 'narrow perceptions of beauty' in human making that limited it to 'the fields of painting and sculpture'.[5] There are clear similarities with the arguments William Morris made from the 1870s for good design in all products in the home, which effectively gave everyone a share in art and enhanced the general beauty of life. Nikolaus Pevsner thus called Morris a pioneer of modern design in that 'we owe it to him that an ordinary man's dwelling house has become once more a worthy object of the architect's thought, and a chair, a wallpaper or a vase a worthy object of the artist's imagination'.[6]

The idea of improving the stock of beauty in one's home through acquiring a range of well-designed products is a ubiquitous sales pitch from high-end design and fashion magazines like *World of Interiors*, *Vogue*, *Dwell*, and *Cabana* to IKEA's marketing.[7] Still, designers continue to express a larger claim about the purpose of their work designing our everyday domestic lives. It is another expression of the design apology, namely that good design in our everyday, domestic surroundings goes beyond momentary and fashionable lifestyle choices, dependent on our incomes, to creating the conditions necessary for everyday aesthetic lives. But can a private domestic life really be designed? Should it be even? These questions challenge how designers use notions of need, function, and aesthetic experience in contexts beyond the efficacy of individual products. I examine answers provided by Scandinavian design, as well as the idea of how products relate to home life in the work of the Eameses. Also, I look at questions of a social and political character that arise when designing home life, prefiguring overtly utopian design schemes for whole communities, including mass housing.

Aesthetic interiors

The Museum of the Home in London presents domestic objects and arranges them in displays representing typical rooms in homes over the last four hundred years in the UK. While it does so to 'explore how we come to acquire the things that make up our homes and the hidden stories they reveal', the museum also states a purpose that might equally be design's about the home: 'Our purpose is to reveal and rethink the ways we live, in order to live better together.'[8] Like the design apology, the museum's stated vision asserts a significant personal and social value to things of everyday functional use. Designed goods are not simply accumulated because of their specific functionality and the needs that they meet. Together, chosen and arranged in our homes, they represent ideas about the home and ways of living more generally.

In the history and context of design, the ideas associated with late nineteenth-century Aestheticism were central to shifting the idea of good design in products to ideas about ways of living.[9] By 1881, in the UK at least, there was evidence that people generally were interested in 'art' 'not in the Royal Academy [but] ... in our thousand and one shops, and workshops, and manufactories'.[10] The Aesthetic Movement's 'cult of beauty' was seen in the 'decorating choices of a select coterie of artists and intellectuals in 1860s Oxford and Chelsea'.[11] But evidently, it had transferred to design and with that there was the opportunity, for those who could afford it for 'choice, purchase and possession'.[12] Moreover, though, a historian of the Aesthetic Movement concludes it left a 'longer imprint on British and North American domestic and popular culture': its 'utopian visions' were translated 'into a living campaign for better standards of design ... in the soulless working-class environments of the modern industrial city'.[13] William Morris is notable, of course, for combining an aestheticism about product design with social-reforming zeal.

Here, in a nutshell, are a set of themes that play out in various conceptions of the design problem for homes: from '1860s Chelsea' emerge issues about good design and personal self-expression; about social and moral imperatives and the right to choose one's own domestic life; about homes as the loci of a social and political outlook or of individual lifestyle and ostentatious taste. In short, themes that The Museum of the Home asks its visitors to mull over: 'This is a place where everyone can explore what home means. Here you can challenge your own assumptions and consider some of the issues facing our society. It's somewhere we can all think about how we live in the world and look at the world.'[14]

Christopher Dresser worked as 'Art Superintendent' of the Art Furnishers' Alliance' in 1880.[15] It is worth quoting both his role and the company's ambitions based on it because Dresser's role is illustrative of how ideas about good design extended from products to product ranges where the aesthetic functionality of the home became a design aim. Dresser was to be the 'art authority in the company' assessing all its products across the range of furnishing for 'art qualities'.[16] That range extended across house-furnishing including 'furniture, carpets, wall-decorations, hangings, pottery, table-glass, silversmiths' wares, hardware, and whatever is necessary to our household requirements'.[17] Note then the range, the goal of furnishing an entire household, and the aesthetic aims for all products, in themselves and as collectively making a home. No doubt too, companies saw the commercial opportunities offered by Aestheticism's appreciation of the beauty of everyday objects for the home. The Art Furnishers' Alliance was naturally based in London's affluent West End and shops associated with its general ideas were located nearby, like Liberty & Co. and Morris & Co.[18] Indeed, there is perhaps a case for suggesting that the larger department stores that subsequently opened were art galleries of the everyday; alongside later 'ideal home exhibitions', they brought Aestheticism's ideas to the marketplace.[19] Running in parallel, Penny Sparke notes that the period saw new theories and accompanying manuals of interior design appear, broken down to wallpapers, textiles, furniture, ceramics, and metalwork, and more general guides like Eastlake's *Hints on Household Taste*.[20] She also records the growth of magazines and journals dedicated to domestic decoration for both designers and consumers. Soon a special kind of designer emerges, the professional 'interior decorator'. Charting the history of interior design from 1900, 'by the 1920s, a number of influential designers had established themselves successfully, treating the room as a cohesive entity in its own right, rather than as a disparate collection of furniture, fabric and objets d'art'.[21] While these designers worked on single commissions for wealthy clients, the idea, at least, of the room as an aesthetically cohesive space remained part of the utopian aims of Aestheticism. Its delivery though necessitated general ideas about what rooms were *really* for and *should* be like. The first 'Ideal Home Exhibition' in the UK opened in 1908: it reflected a wide range of design interests, from labour-saving devices to effecting social reform through new housing schemes and a new type of home. That the ideal home might be aesthetically driven was also a feature in 1913, for example, when the Omega Workshops – inspired by the artistic ideals of the Bloomsbury Group – exhibited an ideal room.

I also want to note how the idea of an aesthetic interior was thought important to general aesthetic ideals – in that general spirit of good design at the turn of the twentieth century – in the ideas of Charlotte Perkins Gilman. She set out the supposed core needs set by home life and related them to design: 'the home should offer to the individual rest, peace, quiet comfort, health, and that degree of personal expression requisite; and these conditions should be maintained by the best methods of the time'.[22] Gilman's conception of needs is worth noting because it extends to the idea, a version perhaps of the fullest expression of the design apology, that 'the home should be to the child a place of happiness and true development; to the adult a place of happiness and that beautiful reinforcement of the spirit needed by the world's workers'.[23] It does so in that the design apology's key concepts are identified as setting the parameters for the problem of designing a home: what the home should do, the particular needs it should meet; the use of technology; designing for the needs of different people; an overall ambition of happiness and personal and social development. In short, 'to perform our best service to society, and to find our best individual growth and expression; a right home is essential to both these uses'.[24] Her enquiry is about bad design too, into 'conditions which are not necessary, which are directly inimical to the home; and that we shall do well to lay these aside'.[25] It is, then, about the design problems and solutions associated with the home.

Gilman sets these problems in the context of 'domestic art' and the conflict between professional interior designers and individuals managing their own homes. On the one hand, she notes these 'new employments' involved selecting and arranging products to create 'artistic interiors'.[26] On the other hand, Gilman notes 'the lives of half the world', by which she means women, to 'make [the] home beautiful'.[27] Gilman argued that what should be taught was not the new interior design ethos but the inexorable 'laws of applied beauty', which held to the tenets of 'Truth', 'Simplicity', resulting in 'Unity, Harmony', and 'Restraint'.[28] 'In the furnishing and decoration of the home we have room for more harmony than in the exterior, because each room may be treated separately according to its especial purpose'; and there are 'elementary laws which make this thing beautiful, that thing ugly, and the same things vary as they are combined with each other'.[29] With these aesthetic ideals for interiors and believing their capacity to generate similar ways of living for people – truth, simplicity, harmony as human virtues too – Gilman's views are prescient of aspects of modernism's ideas about the proper aims of design for homes.

A machine for living in

In *Towards a New Architecture*, Le Corbusier presented a view of the functionality of the house in a chapter titled 'Airplanes'.[30] He speaks about it in familiar design terms. Albeit in the context of war, Le Corbusier saw that airplane design had necessarily – at the pain of failure and death – 'mobilized invention, intelligence and daring: *imagination* and *cold reason*'.[31] The same spirit 'built the Parthenon'; so why not houses too? What was needed then was for the design problem of the house to be stated. It had not been, at least to Le Corbusier's satisfaction, thus far; and 'the airplane shows us that a problem well stated finds its solution'.[32]

Le Corbusier illustrated the chapter on the problem of the house with images of triplanes that technological advances quickly made obsolete. Can houses be designed in such a technologically driven manner without the same risk? Le Corbusier included a 'Manual of the Dwelling' in the chapter on airplanes that perhaps effectively qualifies the analogy with airplane design. In that, more general requirements for a home are listed that can be met over the long-term like 'a large living room' and 'built-in fittings'.[33] Other statements, however, read like arbitrary decorative advice, or are meaningless without some aesthetic reasoning, like 'Put only a few pictures on your walls and none but good ones'.[34] Others are redundant for the vast majority, like 'demand that the maid's room should not be an attic'.[35] *This* 'machine for living in', at least, is not a general solution to the problem of the house.

Conceptually, however, the idea of designing a home room by room as a set of problems of functionality in each and for the whole house chimes with the design apology's ideas about human flourishing. This was immediately apparent to designers concerned with poor social housing and slum clearance in the 1920s and 1930s. And where they remain issues, so the 'machine' concept sets a benchmark for approaching the problems. Design problems associated with the house, as Le Corbusier's 'Manual' illustrates, in fact see distinct but overlapping concerns about aesthetic interiors and the general functionality of the mass of houses. For example, built-in cupboards, open planning, and utilitarian furniture, set a general functional standard for housing but clearly also engage aesthetic considerations about the kind of experiential life they engender. But I focus here on the home as a place for an individual household, and on housing as a social issue in Chapter 6.

Still, when considering the house-machine concept of the 1920s and 1930s in Europe at least, it is necessary to understand it is an aesthetic functionalism about the home driven by a design problem set in terms of meeting the needs of most urban dwellers for decent living conditions.[36] The background is an existing housing stock of industrial slums. In the UK Anthony Bertram followed Le Corbusier's lead (*Towards A New Architecture* was first published in English in 1927) with *The House: A Machine for Living In*. It outlined 'the design of the house-machine as a whole in relation to its various chief functions, and the design and equipment of each part in relation to its particular function'.[37] While acknowledging that at certain times certain parts of the house fulfil many functions, Bertram's fundamental approach is analytic rather than organic: 'The chief functions of the house are to satisfy the needs of shelter, eating, sleeping, recreation, health, cleanliness and beauty'.[38] Bertram notes other categories for analysis but puts them outside the scope of his book as 'other important needs' that relate to 'ideas' about 'hospitality, privacy, service, storage and communication'.[39] Still, these are explicable in terms of the core needs; for example, 'hospitality' in terms of 'eating, drinking, and recreation'.

But, even acknowledging a range of functions for the house-machine, are all problems for designers to solve? If they do, and in the engineering spirit of a functional analysis of a house, what kind of home is produced? Bertram is often at pains to counter accusations of wanting to produce cold, comfortless homes akin to 'sitting in a dentist's chair and sleeping on an operating table'.[40] But his solution to counter an austerely functional house-machine is not to rein back on functionalism. The answer is *more* design work. Bertram proposes that while the house-machine view of 'use comes first' remains paramount, good design does not end there.[41] Good design work includes considerations of beauty. Bertram includes beauty as a need in conceiving design problems: 'civilized man has a *need* for comfort and beauty'.[42] At this point in his argument, Bertram again follows lines developed by other design thinkers, particularly Loos on ornamentation. I have noted in Chapter 4 that Bertram followed Loos in arguing that 'plain, unornamented furniture' was the most appropriate form for mass-produced furniture. So, for Bertram, recognizing the need for beauty in design meant letting methods of mass production take care of the form and aesthetic appeal of mass-produced things for the home. It should be noted that, like Loos, Bertram is not oblivious to the history of beautiful objects of everyday use.[43] But in the 'machine age', the only authentic beauty is perfect, plain, unadorned form. It should be noted too, though, that the overlap of design ideas about both the home and social housing meant that every item in a home became subject to that thinking. The 'modernist home' as a mass-produced product, after Le Corbusier, meant designing housing as well as fixtures and fittings. Ernst May is an early example of this in Frankfurt with his 1925–1930 workers' housing, which used 'a number of architects and designers to equip his workers' housing' (Fig. 6).[44] Everything was designed from chairs to stoves and cupboards, which were manufactured and used in thousands of apartments. There were standard plans and details for kitchens and bathrooms too. Demonstration houses at the Weissenhof Siedlung

Figure 6 Kitchen in Ernst May House, 1927–28. Fredrik von Erichsen / dpa picture alliance / Alamy Stock Photo.

exhibition in 1927 epitomize the extent to which domestic life was to be designed on modernist house-machine principles. Tellingly, a poster advertising the exhibition includes the words 'How to live in a dwelling' and a big red cross through a photograph of an ornate nineteenth-century drawing room with fluted columns, artworks in elaborate frames, darkly painted walls, carved gilt French-style chairs, and so on.[45] In contrast, in one house, for example, 'the kitchen was designed along the latest principles to allow a housewife to sit while preparing food, minimizing the movements required while preparing a meal. A hatch allowed food to be passed directly to the living room.'[46]

It is very much in that spirit that ideal homes, at least ideal homes for the mass of urban dwellers, were envisioned, emphasizing hygienic and efficient domestic lives. They were parodied in pictures by William Heath Robinson in the 1930s and in France in Jacques Tati's film *Mon Oncle* in 1958. But mere gadgetry was never modernism's solution to the design problem of the home.

Frank Pick (then chairman of the UK's Council for Art and Industry) set out three fundamental needs associated with the home in his *Maxims for Furnishing*, written for the 1939 Ideal Home Exhibition catalogue. They were: 'You want to be comfortable. You want to realize some sort of life. You want to feel at home yourself.'[47] The general approach is still Le Corbusier's of stating 'the problem of the house'. But crucially the terms of the problem are differently conceived. Importantly, the emphasis is on the experience of living in a home. And that experience is later characterized by Pick beyond the ergonomics of the 'solved' modernist kitchen. I would argue it augments house-machine functionalism, revealing the design apology's essential aesthetic functionalism.

So, Pick's test of comfort is 'usefulness' in basic terms for items of furniture: rigid tables, chairs that support you, wardrobes that keep out dust; in summary, 'convenience and efficiency'.[48] But he adds that, in a home proper, these things also aspire to feelings of a good, pleasurable experiential life. One should question one's furniture like one chooses one's friends: they are both the background of your life, 'the stage upon which you act out your daily life'.[49] Pick continues that 'arrived in your home, an enquiring mind should be able to guess who you are, what you do, what are your politics, your religion or lack of it, your habits, your hobbies, your handiness and skill'.[50] Put on hold the reasonable first thought that this is hardly likely from mass-produced furniture. Pick's maxim about 'realizing a life' unpacks as one about adding personal items ('a special bit') to stock furniture: 'You can change a special bit but let it be a special bit and wear out the ordinary furniture in use without wasting it.'[51] Likewise elaborating on the maxim that you want to feel at home, Pick rightly states that 'you do not want your home to look like a shop window or a model room in a store or a furniture display'.[52] So: 'let the home in a word be yours. Then it will be homely, restful, happy, right.'[53] But really all from furniture plus some personal choices of decoration and enrichment?

And yet Pick regards this combination of good design and the personal touch as embracing the aesthetic in one's domestic life: 'to follow maxims such as these is to follow art, for art is something inherent in life, implicit in work, not to be thought of as difficult or precious or outside, to be sought or purchased'.[54] There are, no doubt, tensions and seeming paradoxes here that highlight issues delivering good design in people's homes beyond the aesthetic functionality of products. Generously perhaps, Pick is clumsily asserting that good design in one's domestic life meets functional needs and is a prerequisite, although not a guarantee, of a comfortable, aesthetic life. His maxims prefigure ideas about designing lifestyles and are a stark contrast to the scientism of house-machine design.

Still, functional modernism with an engineering bias is surely central to designing some interiors like kitchens and bathrooms. It is evidenced, at any rate, in design magazines like *Dwell*. A kitchen design company advertises: 'We obsess over form and function – not unlike

NASA engineers'; and 'We believe everyone deserves a complete, architecturally considered kitchen'; kitchen design that is 'a path to achieving your current and future dreams'.[55] Still, other rooms pose different needs, require different solutions, and fulfil other dreams.

Lifestyles and home futures

In thinking metacritically about design and the home in terms of 'lifestyle', it is important to make a simple distinction between interior design as a practice associated with individual or family affluence and ostentatious good taste, and aspirations it might induce in others, and mass-produced lifestyles. One sufficient reason is that the former includes the acquisition of one-off works of art or rarer products of craftsmanship. A magazine like the *The World of Interiors*, for example, regularly argues for and showcases art and antiques: for example, 'in this issue we consider the wonders and possibilities of living with art and antiques. Frankly, I can't imagine living without either.'[56] The design apology's concern with aesthetic interiors may indeed have origins in the industrial age with the aesthetic interiors of artists' homes. But history aside, design's concern is with how a range of household products, mass-produced and available to most people, might create aesthetic lives in the ordinary home. Again, to highlight the contrast, an issue of *The World of Interiors* included a laudatory article on 'David Hicks on Bathrooms', a book 'washing away set notions of a clinical, functional cubicle' by adding 'high culture' ('art, books, good furniture').[57] In the same issue of the magazine, a description of a bathroom in the home of Geraldine and Leopold Meyer in Paris: 'A Camille Henrot artwork doubles as a functioning radiator. The piles of novels, marble book rest and daybed beneath the porthole window add up to the room as a place of retreat.'[58] Descriptions of items in other rooms are invariably without aesthetic concepts but are 'tables by... (Martin Szekely)', 'sofa by ... (Pierre Paulin)', 'lamp by ... (Wicki Somers)', and so on.

The contrast evidenced by such examples is not just one between art and design though. The implicit idea is that 'high culture' is necessary for a home to achieve any aesthetic effects. Additionally, the choice of cultural artefacts for the home is supposed to reflect the aesthetic sensibilities of the homeowner; and these homes become the proper focus of study of furnishing, for example. This is the view presented by, for example, Mario Praz's 1964 *An Illustrated History of Furnishing* which therefore focuses on wealthy households from ancient Greece to Art Nouveau Paris. Only such homes are really 'a projection of the ego' and worthy of attention.[59]

So, Praz states 'tell me how your house looks and I'll tell you who you are'.[60] When Pick suggested this for everyday homes replete with well-designed, mass-produced furniture, questions of plausibility inevitably arise. Perhaps the doubt is met by considering a democratic design of household products and by extension the home – Scandinavian design – that does present aesthetic values without recourse to art, wealth, and ego.

Four key ideas emerge, I think, from Charlotte and Peter Fiell's overview of Scandinavian design.[61] They are Scandinavian design's: (a) moral basis; (b) focus on household culture; (c) idea of functional pleasures; and (d) social-democratic utopianism.[62]

On its moral basis, the Fiell's claim that 'from its birth around 1920, modern Scandinavian design has been underpinned by a moral humanist ethics ... [a] moral belief in social imperatives that has formed the philosophical bedrock from which Scandinavian design has evolved and prospered'.[63] Be that as it may, designers, even Scandinavian ones, do not require any moral outlook for designing products or normal, everyday use items for the home. The way in which a moral belief in a social ideal – say simply 'democracy' – becomes part of the design problem of an everyday object is not clear.

Perhaps the idea that a chair should be designed that is available to most people sets its design problem in the context of affordability and simplicity (of production, form, and use). But these values are as equally commercial as moral and social values; and once set, they are detached from design work itself: there is no everyday 'moral chair'.

On 'household culture', it is argued that 'for centuries "the home" has been the central focus of the Scandinavian people's existence as it offers not only a vital haven from hostile climatic conditions, but also functions as a framing structure for family life'.[64] But it is doubtful whether there is anything unique to Scandinavian design in thinking that designers work with a 'household culture' in mind. Perhaps placing 'home' in quotation marks properly suggests, though, that the idea of home, while universal, is an open concept where its criteria are different in different times and places.

More interesting is the idea that 'a product – chair, vase, coffee pot or storage jar – . . . should provide an emotional comfort' linked to the concept of *hygge*.[65] This appears, at least, to offer a concrete notion of the experiential value of everyday products that seems to evade writers like Pick and Bertram in a more house-machine vein of thinking. The Fiell's note that Scandinavian products 'express the Scandinavian concept of *hygge* – a Danish word that implies a very special charm, a tender and comfortable feeling'.[66] Things, in other words, that give a sense of joy and well-being. Importantly then, in supporting the design apology's aim to support human experiential flourishing, Scandinavian design aims at pleasures in use, not in possession. There is no value attached to the ostentatious display of good designs. The appeal of good design is not essentially provided by some visual appeal or form, in other words, but is in the experiential value products can afford in a home's sense of fit and well-being. The Fiell's understand this in terms of Scandinavian design's 'soft modernism': the understanding that an industrial aesthetic has alienating effects, and the requirement then to design 'products that put man first, then the machine'.[67] But I think it is reasonable and useful to think in terms of products offering 'functional pleasures'.

So-called 'soft modernism' is evident in this description of the Gunnlogsson House, Rungsted, in Denmark, built in 1958: 'There is evidence of a deep, thoughtful ingenuity at work, one that offers many subtle but functional pleasures, from the sea-chest storage and dressing cabinet in the bedroom to the wall-mounted folding picnic table on the water-facing terrace.'[68] The whole is 'distinctively Scandinavian' but also with influences of 'Asian purity', like a Japanese genkan (entrance) and doors similar to shoji screens.[69] The idea of *hygge* might then, in design terms, be considered a cultural variation on the broader aesthetic concept of 'functional pleasure'.[70] That the concept is broad is illustrated by another interior, the Rams Residence, in Frankfurt, Germany, built in 1971.[71] His design principles for products applied to his 'functional flexible home'; so his home presents 'a way of living made possible by [his] approach to interiors and domestic products'.[72] Compact appliances, and modular and adaptable furniture, for example, allows choice in how one wants to live in the same space from day to day. Rams's home suggests then both functional pleasures and the idea that choice is available to create one's own aesthetic life from and around them. The Eameses proposed a similar philosophy of home design. The 'CSH#8 Eames House, 1945–1949, 203 Chautauqua Boulevard, Pacific Palisades' is described as combining elements of mass production and creative living: 'Although conceived to be prototypical, it is a highly personal reflection of the seamless coexistence of work and leisure characteristic of these prominent American designers' unique way of life.'[73] The idea was expressed in the Eameses' 'House of Cards'. Produced like a conventional deck of cards, individual cards picture familiar products and natural objects and are slotted to enable them to be connected to build structures. The Eameses saw it as representing the possibilities for creative play with designed things. The 'Eameses World' of products then is conceived as one that allows product users to develop their design solutions for their homes. The 'House of Cards' is a useful metaphor for designing the home via household objects. So, it has been argued that while the Eameses maintained a sort of 'remote control' over users by designing the cards and their pictures, 'Eames cannot foresee exact combinations of the cards: it is a choice of the user that organizes each house built by the cards. Eames has found in the picture deck, a design system that permits the creation of other systems. The user's system validates that of the designer.'[74]

Finally on Scandinavian design's social democracy. The Fiell's claim that 'more than anywhere else in the world designers in Scandinavia have instigated and nurtured a democratic approach to design that seeks a social ideal and the enhancement of the quality of life through appropriate and affordable products.'[75] And 'spurred on by the pursuit of a social ideal, Scandinavian designers have consistently provided satisfying design solutions that fulfil both practical and aesthetic requirements, and which are tangible realizations of the five countries' utopian dream.'[76] The observations are no doubt based on a famous 'People's Home' speech by the Swedish social-democrat Per Albin Hansson in 1932. He set out a social-democratic vision of society in which the idea of a 'good home' was central. But the attributes of 'home' were not design-led but related to ideas about the supposed equality, kindness, cooperation, and helpfulness found in the typical home. Still, these attributes could find resonance in product designs for the home which were affordable and functional: in other words, not expensive nor ornate, thus reflecting related political values. In that sense, the social-democratic vision implied, and transferred to, a design-led way of living in the home, a social-democratic lifestyle. Politics had its aesthetic. I examine design's relation to utopian thinking in Chapter 6. Here it is sufficient to conclude that Scandinavian design, when generalized as a set of design principles for living in the home, can however be explained wholly in terms of the idea of functional pleasures.

Another example from the history of design of democratic design principles supporting non-art aesthetic values in the home is provided by Terence Conran and the UK's Habitat furnishing stores. Conran worked as a young man at the 1951 South Bank Exhibition: that exhibition had a role in generating a sense among users that good design in products did not just amount to 'modern convenience' and building a home that had all the mod cons. Conran and Habitat represent the idea of household products being more than just, for example, labour-saving devices; product choices in the home can reflect an artful lifestyle. So, Habitat's first catalogue offered 'instant good taste . . . for switched-on people' and subsequently offered to meet similar aspirations (Fig. 7).[77] The general idea was not new, but the 1960s idiom was, highlighting the role of department stores at the turn of the twentieth century. Sudjic also notes that Conran was copying Scandinavian retailing after visits there in the 1950s: 'the Svenskt Tenn store in Stockholm ... Den Permanente and Illums Bolighus in Copenhagen.'[78] Still, the idea of selling a mass lifestyle is noteworthy for aesthetic functionalism about design. Sudjic reports that while Habitat started as 'the style of choice ... for the young professional setting up home for the first time', it soon became 'the signature style of grown-up Britain'; and then 'the ubiquitous uniform of stylishly affluent suburbia.'[79] He is clearly sceptical then of the opportunities for creative aesthetic lives offered by the Habitat vision: in short, it is good design as mere fashion. Habitat's first store opened in London in 1964 and offered more than furniture: 'it combined European and American modernism ... juxtaposing leather lounge chairs and tubular-steel furniture alongside Japanese paper lanterns . . . Braun consumer electronics.'[80]

But designs, including good ones, are improved upon; change is not mere fashion in that case. This simple fact should allay the depressing conclusion drawn by a recent biographer of Walter Gropius that the legacy of Bauhaus and its art and life ideals – of the design

Figure 7 Habitat Catalogue, 1981/82. PackStock / Alamy Stock Photo.

apology indeed – is no more than a certain kind of furnishing store exemplified by Design Research in the United States, Habitat in the UK, and IKEA internationally.[81] And Scandinavian ideas of home life and Rams's and Eameses' ideals suggest our functional pleasures are worth meeting.

Such reflections on design and the home in twentieth-century thought and practice were part of the UK Design Museum's Home

Futures exhibition in 2018. It addressed that history suggesting that: 'The notion of the "home of the future" as a machine for living was an attempt to modernize domestic life, but it ignored the human need for ritual.'[82] The idea of 'ritual' here is perhaps an acknowledgement already made in Scandinavian and related design about the limits of austere functionalism and the needs that good design properly meets beyond the purely functional requirements set by individual products. But the example used by *Home Futures* of design opposing functionalism is limited itself: 'opposing functionalism, alternative ideas of the domestic realm playfully evoked nature. These dream-like, surreal interiors conjured idyllic landscapes'; 'in the 1970s, designers working with the Italian furniture producer Gufram used polyurethane to produce natural forms, such as a lounge seat shaped like a giant clump of grass and a coat-hanger cactus.'[83] Still, it is stated, design for the home is properly about 'objects that stimulate more emotional or psychological attachments.'[84] But, again, these have been noted as aims of soft modernism at least. *Home Futures* rightly asks: 'Can the dream of efficiency ever respond to our basic human need for comfort, leisure and recreation?'; 'what other ways ... to make our homes better and more fulfilling places to live?'[85] Yet again, the answers might lie in the best aims and efforts of good design in the twentieth century, and in an understanding of the full meanings of the design apology.

Of course, *Home Futures* is correct too to note changes in conceptions of the family and in technology. So, 'new family constellations are becoming more common, challenging the traditional nuclear family.'[86] There are 'urban nomads', for example, needing little more than their smartphone and laptop. But these situations just require reworking design problems around different conceptions of 'family' and with new technologies in mind.

Digital technology as a whole no doubt also adds a new dimension to thinking about the home of the future. It is explored, for example, by the design company Maio, an architectural office based in Barcelona and New York. They present a manifesto for the 'Diffuse House', not dissimilar in style and tone to Le Corbusier's one hundred years before. Without additional comment, I quote as an example of how an open concept like the 'home', set in whatever technological conditions pertain at the time, necessarily invites radical conceptions of design problems:

> The diffuse house operates 24/7. The diffuse house is ubiquitous. The diffuse house is networked . . . The diffuse house is a factory, an office, a workstation, a workshop, and a home, among others. The diffuse house relies on immaterial economies. . . Within the diffuse house, public and private spheres converge . . . The diffuse house does not have dwellers but performers.[87]

Aesthetic functionalism about designing the home superficially resembles Gaston Bachelard's about the 'poetics of space' when he argues that the 'dream' in 'dream home' is not the dream of ownership but *to dream*, to create a life: 'the dream house must possess every virtue. . .'. But it is rightly argued that while Bachelard appeals to good designers in those terms, his 'design solution' is merely nostalgic.[88] Indeed, Bachelard continues that 'however spacious, it [the dream home] must also be a cottage, a dove-cote, a nest'.[89] The 'Diffuse House' example illustrates otherwise and drives new 'dream home' solutions, new 'home futures'.

Conclusion

The Museum of the Home was called the Geffrye Museum: its change of name in 2021 indicated a change in aims for the museum. While still presenting a historical record of UK rooms, the displays are now made with the intention of raising questions in visitors about how to live well. The change perhaps reflects a general change in design's ideas about its role in designing the home. It is at least symbolic of a move from the various attempts through the history of design to conceive the 'ideal' home – in its broadly artistic (Aestheticism), moral (Gilman), functional (Le Corbusier), economic and political (social-democratic utopian), and lifestyle (Conran) versions – to variegated thinking about what the home is for and what we mean by living well in one.

But if product design flows into product ranges based on ideas of domestic living and not just single product functionality, then design still aims at ordered, flourishing, general domestic activities: to ideas of harmonious home life – however 'home' is conceived – and its functional pleasures. The design apology's aesthetic ambitions for the home, then, are not about establishing critical artistic taste in interior design choices by people. Moreover, they are ones associated with also creating conditions for creative aesthetic lives, after the ideas of Dieter Rams and the Eameses, for example. The design apology's 'dream home' is one where good design's functional pleasures also unleash, by example and by releasing us from a wholly functional life, a 'hands-on improvisatory and innovative' life.[90] Then again, some designers have something additional in mind thinking about good housing: so, the idea of the home as part of planning housing estates and cities is the subject of Chapter 6.

6

Designing communities and the good life

Introduction

Examples like Ebenezer Howard's *Garden Cities of To-Morrow*, the UK's New Towns, social housing estates, and planned urban areas across the world have all tested the design apology's utopian aspirations for city living. Ideas of slum clearance are laudable of course – of design used to improve basic living conditions – and were the stock-in-trade of early and mid-twentieth-century city-based, designed utopias. Now in the twenty-first century, core functional design problems for urban planning relate primarily to environmental sustainability and energy consumption. But can friendship and neighbourliness in urban living be designed, happiness even, alongside these functional requirements? Are ideas about 'smart cities of the future' aesthetic at all? I argue that aesthetic understanding of need, function, and flourishing in the design apology applied to communities suggest what can reasonably be expected of good design.

Utopias

Presenting the New Towns bill to the UK parliament in 1946, the Minister of Town and Country Planning, Lewis Silkin, stated: 'Cicero said: A man's dignity is enhanced by the home he lives in. I say, even more by the town he lives in. In the long run, the new towns will be judged by the kind of citizens they produce, by whether they create this spirit of friendship, neighbourliness, and comradeship. That will be the real test.'[1] The minister was also evoking the spirit if not the precise plans of Thomas More's *Utopia* and Ebenezer Howard's *Garden Cities of To-Morrow* (Fig. 8). Howard set this aim for designers in 1898: 'reconstructing anew the entire external fabric of society'.[2] Fifty years later, its idea to lay the foundations for a new 'urban civilization' was commended by Lewis Mumford. He thought that these foundations, their design, were 'needed for biological survival and economic efficiency [and] likewise lead to social and personal

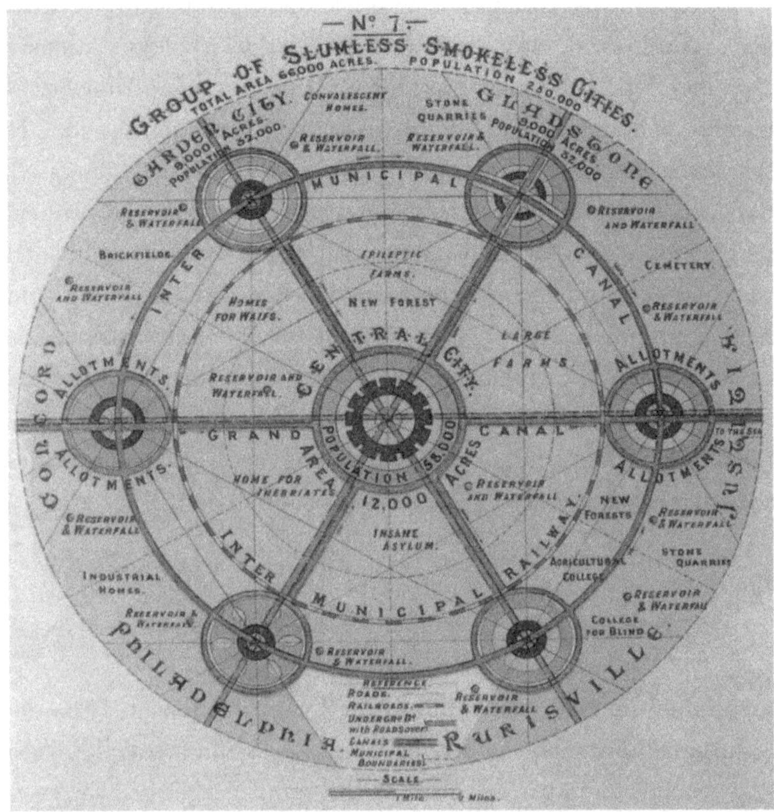

Figure 8 Garden City plan, Ebenezer Howard, 1898. Public Domain via Wikimedia Commons.

fulfilment'.[3] These are general themes throughout design's history of designing communities; in the twenty-first century, they are reconfigured around environmental sustainability and circularity, energy use, and ideas about social living, but about 'happy cities' too.

Silkin was surely right to caution that such utopian claims – 'enhanced dignity', 'social and personal fulfilment', and so on – must be tested. In the decades that followed Silkin's speech, the test was failed, if this is to go by: a description of 'Utopia' from a dictionary of design: 'the utopian ideals of the planners and architects who built housing in Britain during the post-war era are now considered to be outdated and, in some areas, disastrous. The rapid demise of the society they tried to create led to the creation of Utopia's opposite, dystopia, which described the crime-ridden estates their visions had become.'[4] Publicly funded mass housing, part of the utopian aspiration, in the UK – 'council housing' – has an inauspicious history, inadvertently but neatly summed up in adjoining index entries to a book on that history: 'utopianism' and 'vandalism'.[5]

An example is the story of the Quarry Hill estate in Leeds. The front cover of Anthony Bertram's 1938 *Design* shows a model of the modernist estate, then the largest social housing estate in the UK and under construction. Bertram described it as 'a social unit with shops, playgrounds, assembly hall, schools etc.'[6] It had featured in a 1930s government information film 'Housing Problems', seen as the design solution to the problems of overcrowding and insanitary conditions of Victorian industrial dwellings. Quarry Hill was demolished in 1978. It was not alone in that fate. For example, the demolition in the 1970s of the Pruitt-Igoe housing estate of thirty-three modernist high-rise blocks built in the 1950s in St. Louis in the United States was announced at the time as the 'death of modern architecture' by the architectural theorist Charles Jencks (Fig. 9).[7] Like many estates, they had become prey to issues around social behaviours from individual tenants and to issues with maintenance staff and local authorities

Figure 9 Pruitt-Igoe housing demolition, 1972. Maidun Collection / Alamy Stock Photo.

managing estates. They failed, in other words, in the broader context of socio-economic conditions, especially associated with the urban poor. Le Corbusier had concluded from his understanding of the design problem of the house that 'Men – intelligent, cold and calm – are needed to build the house and to lay out the town.'[8] This contrast between the cold, intelligent designer of towns and housing and ordinary people living in them is starkly illustrated by Anthony Bertram's observations: 'we must not be disappointed because some tenants complain, because here and there things go wrong . . . we must remember we are building for the future as for the present. And as some unlucky people have been conditioned by their slum surroundings into slovenly ways, so the coming generations can be conditioned by good surroundings into the good life.'[9]

Bertram's view of conditioning responses to modern housing foresaw problems like those at Quarry Hill but clearly trusted to good design in the long run. His top-down view is tempered perhaps by his comment that it is the 'trees and grass and bricks and mortar of a well-planned and imaginative estate' that do such work.[10] Here is the suggestion that the good designer of a whole community – which was the intended scope of large housing estates and new towns – must address aesthetic as well as purely functional needs. So Silkin clearly states:

> Our towns must be beautiful. Here is a grand chance for the revival or creation of a new architecture. The monotony of the interwar housing estate must not be repeated. We must develop in those who live in the towns, an appreciation of beauty. I am a firm believer in the cultural and spiritual interest of beauty. The new towns can be experiments in design as well as in living. . . I believe that if all these conditions are satisfied, we may well produce in the new towns a new type of citizen, a healthy, self-respecting, dignified person with a sense of beauty, culture and civic pride.[11]

I quote at length because, despite the failures, the design of communities persists with such utopian aspirations for the everyday lives of people: that is, with design aims set beyond meeting basic human needs and intent on some vision of human flourishing. The 'city of the future' is a perennial design problem because of its broadly aesthetic, everyday experiential conception, which necessarily engages designers with thoughts of new and imaginative design solutions to problems of 'how to live'.[12]

It is unsurprising then that Rosemary Wakeman starts her intellectual history of the New Town movement (especially associated with the period after the end of the Second World War) with the observation that 'there is nothing new about new towns'.[13] Most notably, she notes that the ancient Romans were 'master town builders'.[14] Wakeman's concept of 'new' is used to 'denote deliberate and highly symbolic acts of territorial control and settlement'; with each new town 'acting as a brand, an image of the future, a step into a new era'.[15] She adds that in planning new towns a general idea prevailed that 'how a town was designed and laid out, how it was built, how society would function inside it, could be deciphered by anyone living within or passing through its precincts'.[16] Another way to put this is to state that designers conceive the problem of building new towns or urban areas with ideas about *how society should* function. And to that end, designers are concerned with establishing the needs of people living in these places.

With that understanding, the first book on architectural principles by Vitruvius in the first century BCE is about more than architectural style. Indeed, it explicitly prefaces preferred styles with a list of the fundamental human needs a (Roman) city must meet: they are familiar ones of health, security, and safety, mass housing, and public and private spaces. Vitruvius also considered public buildings for specific purposes like temples. Now, the equivalents would be our opera houses, museums, and art galleries. These buildings raise questions about aesthetics and architecture, of course. But my focus is on public buildings and planning on a mass scale, on designing communities. In Vitruvius's division of architecture into 'departments', 'designing communities' is perhaps most closely linked to 'the construction of fortified towns and of works for general use in public places'.[17] Also, Vitruvius outlined the origins and development of dwelling houses, and it is noteworthy that public housing was to be designed with 'due reference to durability, convenience, and beauty'.[18] And, for all building projects, the health of the whole site of a city should be in mind.[19]

By establishing architectural principles in the holistic context of a city's proper functioning, Vitruvius effectively presents a utopian vision of the city. At least, his descriptions of the general layout of a city, the functions of different parts and buildings, and the needs that are met, all chime with Thomas More's characterization of the cities of *Utopia*. So, for example, in More's utopian city, design meets basic functional requirements so that 'the streets are laid out to facilitate traffic and to offer protection from the wind'.[20] But More, like Vitruvius, also thinks that 'beauty' is a design aim. I list these quotes to illustrate: 'the buildings are by no means ugly'; 'the houses extend in a continuous row along the whole block': 'behind the houses, a large garden . . . the Utopians place great stock by these gardens'; 'there is no house which does have a door opening on the street and a backdoor into the garden'; 'the double doors, which open easily with a push of the hand and close again automatically, allow anyone to come in'.[21] These design aims and features are not simply functional. More is thinking about designing a city that offers experiential value to its citizens: so, of the gardens, 'you will not see any feature of the whole city that is of greater use to the citizens or gives them more pleasure'.[22] I note one more thing relating utopian planning with ideas about good design, that More indicated that the design of cities in *Utopia* left scope for change and improvement: the 'designer' 'left it to succeeding ages to complete the adornment and landscaping'.[23] More suggested, then, that new materials and technologies would be embraced over time, so that while the city plan remained, houses would get, in his terms, more handsome and bigger, use fireproof and weather-resistant materials, use more glass, and so on. More's description of a *Utopian* city expresses fundamental design concerns about communities and housing, like the use of materials and technologies, the quality of homes and their fittings, about how places develop over time, and about the needs of users being met in experientially pleasurable and valuable ways.

By the time design was establishing itself as a distinct profession in the nineteenth century, ideas about designing communities were necessarily set against an increasingly industrialized and urban landscape. Industrial cities had not developed in planned ways.[24] Nor had utopian aspirations about the general quality of life in cities any hold. Designers like William Morris railed against this, applying principles of the good design of products to ideas about the best design of communities. But Morris's carefree, bucolic, craft-led vision of the future in his utopian novel *News from Nowhere* hardly dealt with the immediate needs of city-dwellers.

Still, the idea that the aims of good design should extend to the lives of the urban poor – to improving basic living conditions *and* making people happy – found concrete expression in Ebenezer Howard's 'Garden City' concept. He thought the primary need was 'to restore the people to the land'.[25] This was not an agricultural demand, though, but a romantic ideal of nature's beauty pouring 'a flood of light on the [urban] problems of intemperance, of excessive toil, of restless anxiety, of grinding poverty'.[26] Howard thought that his designs for a new co-equal town-country would retain the opportunities for social intercourse of crowded cities but also 'the beauties of nature may encompass and enfold each dweller therein'; 'beautiful homes and gardens may be seen on every hand', with the result being 'a happy people'.[27] Reiterating the experiential goal of this new type of city, Howard claims that the newly designed fabric of society would create 'a new sense of freedom and joy' in the hearts of people, 'a social life which permits alike of the completest concerted action and of the fullest individual liberty' and 'reconciliation between order and freedom – between the well-being of the individual and of society'.[28] Howard challenged the idea that new designs for town and country were implausible in old, settled countries with their towns and cities built. His appeal is to the power of real human needs forcing new adaptations: 'each generation should build to suit its own needs'.[29] Protecting cities was, he argued, analogous to protecting the stage-coach system when challenged by the railways.

As with Vitruvius and More, Howard's grand design for a new type of city was grounded on ideas of both meeting basic human needs and their contribution to a larger aim of freer, happier lives led in beautiful surroundings. Into the twentieth century at least, designers are invigorated by the design apology at its furthest reach: designing communities and the good life in terms that are both functional and aesthetic.[30]

A leading example, of course, is the Bauhaus, formed in 1919 out of existing German Arts and Crafts and fine arts organizations and designated an Institute of Design in 1926. It combined 'romantic socialist and utopian aspirations'.[31] So, its aims were no less than this: 'Together let us desire, conceive, and create the new structure of the future'.[32] Bauhaus aimed to educate designers, artists, and craftspeople to the extent that they 'will know how to design buildings harmoniously in their entirety – structure, finishing, ornamentation, and furnishing'.[33] The range and integration of this design work is found in examples like the Torten Housing Estate of affordable homes in Dessau (1926–28) where patterned wallpaper and fabrics, furniture, and the houses and estate itself were all designed by Bauhaus.[34] The link from 'chairs' to 'utopia' was not, then, inconceivable for modernist product designers in the 1920s. As Sudjic notes: 'they wanted to remake familiar domestic objects in radically new forms to make a point about the modern world', and though 'they might not be able actually to build utopia', they designed chairs from metal that 'hinted at what a utopian machine age might one day look like'.[35] Certainly, there is evidence to support this account of how modernist designers conceived their design work in, for example, the pronouncements of Adolf Loos. He believed he had 'discovered' that 'the evolution of culture comes to the same thing as the removal of ornament from functional objects'.[36] Moreover, that: 'Behold, the time is at hand. Fulfilment awaits us. Soon the streets of the cities will gleam like white walls!'[37] Examples of that spirit – connecting utopianism with architectural visions for urban spaces – abounded in post-WWI Europe especially. For example, Kate Arnaud identifies a group called the Crystal Chain, who were architects and artists led by the architect and design theorist Bruno Taut, who shared utopian visions. They produced 'a body of work … closer to the expressive forms of an illustrated science fiction novel rather than an architectural portfolio'.[38] Arnaud argues that the Crystal Chain redressed the balance with the 'austere functionalism' that followed them in the 1920s, with ideas of an architecture that is 'experimental, extravagant and prophetic, ushering in an entirely new mode of living'.[39] The latter idea, however, was not confined to 'paper architects' and avant-garde visionaries. It was, as noted here, integral to Bauhaus ideals, as well as evident in Loos's arguments against unnecessary ornamentation and Le Corbusier's for new designs for the machine age and its new way of living.

Before looking in more detail at the 'fulfilment' of utopian aspirations in mass housing projects, it is worth noting too that ideas about the 'future city' remain linked to experimental, 'paper paradise' architecture. Charting that history from 1956 to 2006, for example, a book accompanying an exhibition of these plans has headings that include 'experimental living', 'concept city', 'the oblique city', 'inflatable city', 'organic city', 'new urban habitat', and 'new babylon'.[40] 'New

Babylon' by Constant Nieuwenhuys is noted as the first global city project, and yet Nieuwenhuys was neither an architect nor a city planner but an artist: 'Anticipating the contemporary era of global communication, Constant's vast meta-city, realized in countless maquettes, drawings and photomontages, is populated by inhabitants who are constantly on the move.'[41] The artist had based his global city on the single idea that 'we are all nomads now', influenced by the French philosopher Guy Debord's situationist ideas.[42]

I want to use a related example of combined design and politically motivated utopian thinking to draw an important distinction between aesthetic and political visions of future cities. It confirms that the design apology's aim for human flourishing can be, and is properly, conceived independently of political values and ideals. But it also illustrates how design and political aims for cities sometimes get enmeshed. Through the 1950s, 1960s, and early 1970s, especially in France, design gets embroiled in intellectual disputes carried out in talks, interviews, and journal articles, relating politics to architecture, urbanism, and what the philosopher Henri Lefebvre called 'the production of space'. Lefebvre was commissioned by the sociologist Mario Gaviria to produce a research document on Spain's Mediterranean leisure industry, specifically Benidorm, exploring the idea of tourist centres as 'laboratories of the employment of free time': the result was *Toward an Architecture of Enjoyment*.[43] Both Gaviria and Lefebvre thought the traditional political left was too ascetic in its understanding of such resorts; and it also acted as a counter to the perceived austere functionalism of modernist-inspired urban planning.

In summary, Lefebvre used the Benidorm study to advance arguments about designing places with *jouissance* ('pleasure') as the goal: in short, 'an architecture devoted to happiness'.[44] This type of architecture means the architect is neither an engineer nor an artist, but a 'concrete utopian' concerned with 'lived experience'.[45] Lefebvre also mocks the architecture of 'needs', both at city and domestic levels. Rather, design's core functional requirement is delivering enjoyment; it 'allows it, leads to it, prepares it'.[46] But what is this idea of design's utopian aspirations grounded in? First, it seems, a basic anti-functionalism: 'No signs!'; second, the 'theory of moments': 'the space of enjoyment cannot consist of a building ... [by] places determined by their functions... Rather it will be ... moments, encounters, friendships, festivals ... play'.[47] So, the key design debate for Lefebvre in the 1960s was with Guy Debord about how the 'moment' is best explained and lived. Perhaps there are interesting philosophical connections here with John Dewey's account of aesthetic experience and its 'consummatory moments'. But the point at issue is how any political ideal of authentic living, even couched philosophically, conspires against design work proper. Design problems are no longer conceived as needs present themselves (perhaps signs are needed in some places, as Saito argued in Chapter 3!). Lukasz Stanek's introduction to Lefebvre's book on enjoyment indeed records that speculative projects to improve mass housing by adopting a more leisure-oriented approach did occur. For example, the magazine *Actuel* (No. 12, September 1971) published a 'revised and corrected Quartier d'Italie' suggesting a plastic bubble, murals, a Swiss chalet, an 'old house', and so on, as correctives to this modern Parisian housing estate.[48] Clearly this was not essentially a redesign with residents' needs in mind, not a genuine rethinking of the design problem for urban housing.

Still, the design apology is concerned with everyday issues associated with long commuting times, the absence of green spaces in urban housing estates, and now more besides, that were addressed in the context of *jouissance* by French politicians in the early 1970s. Lefebvre's political ideals happen to accord, despite his caricaturing of needs-driven design, with the design apology's general goals of well-being. But it is a fine line. I briefly note Lefebvre and French philosophical politics to illustrate an important distinction that emerges for a true philosophical understanding of good design. That is one between the language of order, harmony, and flourishing or happiness used for conceiving design problems and that used as a means of statecraft. The design apology's utopianism is aesthetic in so far as its notion of the good everyday life is personal, experiential, and creative. It contrasts with political conceptions of 'beauty' – effectively co-opting the design apology – as social cohesion, political unity, and collective experience. Good design enables everyday aesthetic lives: the beauty of buildings and the city are evidenced in the quality of the lives led in and around them, not in how they reflect political ideals.

Mass housing and urban planning

The Werkbund, a precursor of the Bauhaus, was an organization of businesses, artists, architects, and designers, founded in Germany in 1907, with a programme that encapsulates one aspect of the design apology, its range of design interests: 'from producing a tiny sofa cushion to the construction of cities'.[49] The 1927 Werkbund exhibition called 'The Dwelling' included an experimental housing estate of thirty-three multifamily and single-family buildings, detached and terraced, as well as sixty-three model flats.[50] It was designed in the intellectual, avant-garde atmosphere of talk of the 'Neues Bauen', the 'New Flat'. So, Ludwig Mies van der Rohe wrote in the Stuttgart exhibition's literature: 'Problems of the "New Flat" result from the changed material, social and intellectual conditions of our time; only from this perspective can these problems be understood... the problem of housing is basically an intellectual problem, and the fight for the New Flat is only part of a wider battle for new forms of living'.[51]

Even an avowed anarchist like Herbert Read – who in that vein stressed above all else aesthetically, 'the importance of living' – could succumb to the supposed 'abstract art' and aesthetic value conveyed by an aerial photograph of a housing estate in the Werkbund spirit and style at Dammerstock, Karlsruhe, in Germany.[52] He compared it favourably with a photograph of an assembly of engineering units comprising the B-amplifier output switching relays at Broadcasting House, London: 'the resemblance between these two illustrations is not merely fortuitous; the same laws of design end in the same effects of harmony'.[53] Read also compared an Alvar Aalto designed office with the C-amplifier bays at Broadcasting House, again suggesting that while 'entirely different problems are being solved ... the same absolute sense of order and harmony presides over each functional fulfilment'.[54] Read mistakes external, visual aesthetic effects of harmony as necessarily marking successful design solutions. The aesthetic order and harmony that matter for a housing estate and an office *qua* design are not static and visual but lived and experienced. So, Read has insufficient, at best, empirical grounds for asserting that the estate and office have fulfilled their functional requirements by their visual appeal alone. And what Mies van der Rohe's 'new form of living' amounts to must remain unclear if only the exteriors of buildings are evaluated, rather than the experiences of living in them. Read is insistent, though, that abstract artists like Mondrian and Ben Nicholson (at the time he was writing) effectively act as 'pure artists' for the use of industrial design, in a relation akin to that of pure to applied mathematics.[55] The spell under which Read seems to be cast – that 'artistic' design determines form and trumps judging the live aesthetic experience of things and places – remains an issue for good design.[56]

Countering Read's view of urban planning and housing based on abstract aesthetic principles, the architectural critic Lewis Mumford commended a different kind of aesthetic, urban planning. In doing so he also provided some criteria for the quality of life lived in estates he commended. One attracted his attention. The Lansbury estate 'replaced a packed slum with a reduced density, low-rise development of small residential clusters focused on green spaces, primary schools, and a new district centre with shops, pubs and a market'.[57] The first part of its development was a living architecture exhibit at the 1951 Festival of Britain.

Mumford's views link the utopianism of Howard, for example, and the best examples of low-rise modernism, with ideas now current about smart, happy cities. Mumford praised the Lansbury Estate in Poplar, East London, explicitly contrasting it with Le Corbusier's 'abstract' designs: 'Its design has been based not solely on abstract aesthetic principles, or on the economics of commercial construction, or on the techniques of mass production, but on the social constitution of the community itself, with its diversity of human interests and human needs.'[58] Similarly, there is an emphasis on good design necessarily meeting needs: Lansbury is 'a fresh form based on a traditional pattern but reinterpreted in terms of modern needs'.[59] For Mumford it contrasted with some of modernism's 'sternly hygienic' and 'barracks architecture'; with 'the clichés of "high rise" building' and 'the dreary prisonlike order that results from forgetting the very purpose of housing and the necessities of neighbourhood living'.[60] Mumford compares Lansbury favourably with Ernst May's 1930s housing estate in Römerstadt, Frankfurt am Main; and unlike Read can do so on aesthetic grounds related to the experience of living there, rather than on photographs. For Mumford, design's aim was a successful experiential result: 'the social constitution of the community itself, with its diversity of human interests and human needs'.[61]

Still, Mumford surely caricatures Le Corbusier's modernism and housing design. His Unite d'habitation in Marseilles was commissioned by the French state, with construction beginning in 1946. Its conceptual background in ideas of communal living share something with Mumford's concern for neighbourliness and community. It was 'designed as a "vertical garden city"', not a 'barracks'.[62] Local amenities were addressed: there were mid-air streets with shops, a nursery school, and a gymnasium. All combined with mass-produced furniture by Charlotte Perriand, including features like built-in cupboards. And yet, later in the twentieth-century, concerns began about the mental health of its occupants and 'the people of Marseilles nicknamed the building in their local dialect the "Maison du Fada" the madhouse'.[63] And ultimately, the design apology in relation to building communities rests, of course, on well-being.

When Indian Prime Minister Nehru determined on a new capital city for the Punjab in northern India after its independence from British colonial rule, it was with socio-political goals at the forefront. The city, Chandigarh, was 'a new town planned from A–Z', designed to proclaim India's modernity, its new, modern ways of living.[64] Moreover, Nehru envisioned that young, Indian architects and wider Indian society might learn ideas and techniques of modern design in the process of planning and building the city.[65] Nehru trusted that 'our creative genius' would also come into play.[66] By 1951 Le Corbusier had taken charge of the master plan. In the process, he had invited Indian government officials to see his Marseilles housing project with its, at least superficially, similar social and modernizing design goals. Le Corbusier wrote that 'the experiences gained in Marseilles … were here applied in their purest form'.[67] But he also noted that as a political capital, Chandigarh's main design problem was constructing a 'Capitol', an area containing government buildings. Indeed, his main architectural work was designing these buildings – an Assembly, High Court, and Secretariat – and their position in an overall plan of the city. Housing was largely left with fellow designers, especially Maxwell Fry, Jane Drew, and Pierre Jeanneret.[68] Vinayak Bharne notes that when Le Corbusier took over from Albert Meyer's brief planning leadership in 1951, curved streets became an orthogonal grid and 'Villages' were redesigned and designated as 'Sectors'; and the Capitol Complex was placed at some distance from the rest of the city, designed as a monument to the nation, part of the 'official' rather than 'free' sector of the city.[69] Additionally, Maristella Casciato notes that Le Corbusier's ultimate control of Chandigarh was bound to design principles he had already established in 'highly theoretical texts'.[70] It is those texts and the experiential problems they have been argued to create that concern the philosophical aesthetics of design. The absence of intimacy and the sense of monumentalism about Chandigarh seem to resonate with the experiences of residents of the Unite d'habitation in Marseilles, also as noted a state commission with high-minded social ideals for which Le Corbusier's design principles seemed the perfect match.

So, for example, Sharon Irish has written about her experience living in Chandigarh in 1999 in terms of the contrast between Le Corbusier's Capitol and a rock garden also designed and built privately in the city in the 1950s.[71] She does so based on two images of Le Corbusier's Assembly building; and on her experiences of visiting the garden. The two images show a 'contrast between the curving, unplanned path that pedestrians have made as they leave the bottom of the ramp [to Le Corbusier's Assembly Hall], and the axial, monumental path implicit in the organization of the large concrete plaza in front of the Assembly Hall'.[72] They are meant to reveal that 'Le Corbusier's monumentalism … was imposed on Chandigarh's landscape and the inhabitants with the assumption that he knew best'.[73] Irish contends that while one can admire the buildings in the Capitol Complex, they are not built for 'intimate relationships'.[74] Indeed, the Complex 'dwarfs the individual or remains empty of life, much like an ancient archeological site'.[75] Contrast that with her experience of the Rock Garden, begun as a private project by Nek Chand Saini in 1958 but opened to the public since 1976: its influences are from the vernacular architecture of rural northern India. Irish also notes the similar observations of Chandigarh resident and architect Madhu Sarin that 'Chandigarh is showing signs of becoming a monument to one man's perceived vision of a tidied-up society'.[76] Irish concludes that Chandigarh's Corbusian planning offered no opportunities for experimentation and evolution; and that the solution is to add other functions to the Capitol like shops, and cultural and recreation areas.[77]

It is moot whether Irish offers a meaningful contrast given the radically different needs associated with government buildings and gardens.[78] But Le Corbusier certainly invites, at least, related criticism about top-down town planning and its relations to the everyday experiential lives of people. And that criticism, in terms of intimacy, pure functionality, and the supposed creative vision that justifies a master plan, are factors indicated by Irish and Sarin. It is a criticism perhaps reinforced by an artistic defence of Le Corbusier, like one that suggests that 'the Capitol in Chandigarh seems to pull the vast Indian sky down to earth and to launch the eye towards the foothills of the Himalayas. This ensemble is both a cosmic landscape and a piece of "land art".'[79] Such an architectural experience of Chandigarh seems only to validate arguments that Le Corbusier's design principles put a grand vision and an associated artistic sensitivity and appreciation before people's everyday aesthetic, urban lives.

Turning then to Le Corbusier's 'highly theoretical texts', *Aircraft*, with its 'bird's eye view' of urban planning, seems most evidently to support the argument that Chandigarh's lack of aesthetic intimacy is rooted in a particular way of conceiving design problems for cities.[80] Le Corbusier's conception is not argued as such but a combination of maxims, slogans, and photographs. Some quotes indicate its flavour: for example, a section headed 'The Bird's Eye View' reveals Le Corbusier's city-planning ethos is based on the view from an aircraft, a general aerial view that 'established a new standard of measurement' and a 'new basis of sensation'.[81] 'Man will make use of it to conceive new aims. Cities will arise out of their ashes.'[82] For Le Corbusier, 'The Airplane Indicts the City'.[83] So, aerial photographs of London, Paris, and Berlin are supposed to indicate cities built with only one function in mind, namely 'to make money'.[84] Furthermore, 'cities must be extricated from their misery ... come what may. Whole quarters of them must be destroyed and new cities built'.[85] And the book ends with the quote, 'the flock needs a shepherd'.[86] The language and imagery of destruction not development and of a single designer with a bird's eye view in charge of all aspects of urban living contrives to caricature Le Corbusier. But despite his 'bird's eye view', Le Corbusier is not city-planning's Harry Lime, insensitive to the human 'dots' on the ground, each insignificant in the context of bigger schemes.[87] Rather, Le Corbusier raises legitimate general issues about urban living, about space, light, air quality, about the experience of living in cities.[88] If insufficiencies are properly noted in the experience of living in Chandigarh, then what is at issue is the proper conception of the design problems of specific cities. That properly involves analysing people's complex experiential needs in cultural settings, including those related to community and intimacy, in addition to meeting the design problems set by universal, human needs of city living, like those reasonably identified in the 1920s by Le Corbusier. In that context Bharne finds scope to conclude that Chandigarh, 'envisioned by a great leader, conceived by a great architect' might be seen 'then as an unfinished utopia'.[89] Removed of its guise as a local 'ruin' and no longer merely witness to some Corbusian design conceit, there are opportunities to strip the city of its 'Corbusian veils' and evolve beyond that identity.[90]

In the section 'Smart, happy cities', I consider the broader issues that are raised in the twenty-first century about city planning that wishes to hold to the utopian ideals of the design apology while respecting the ultimate test of the experiential quality of everyday, urban lives. But I briefly note here that design issues raised by Chandigarh resonate with designers in India still. So, for example, government plans to demolish traditional chawl housing in Mumbai and replace with modern tower blocks is challenged on various grounds that also challenge a Corbusian planning view. Such 'all-or-nothing' thinking is disputed, and it is argued that 'architects need to be seen as mediators, and work together with other groups to build consensus'.[91] Questions are raised about transformation rather than demolition, while acknowledging that existing housing is poor. Elsewhere, in Ladakh in northern India, Oorvi Sharma argues that local, idiosyncratic identities should be maintained, especially ones that 'sustain ancient knowledge of ecological stewardship'.[92] And that means town planning is not left only to the state and planning professionals. It is a model that expressly runs counter to Le Corbusier and to Nehru's vision too of 'imported planning ideologies' and imposed modernism.[93] In terms of the general design apology, these examples can be reasonably understood as (re)asserting the primacy of user and environmental needs, and the experiential tests they infer, in mass housing and urban planning.

London's East End around the Lansbury estate – the supposed anti-Corbusian model of urban planning argued by Mumford – did not develop on Lansbury's lines. Instead, high-rise and high-density flats were built. The futuristic outlook of architects Alison and Peter Smithson pictured in their 'space age' apartment prevailed.[94] Their 1972 Robin Hood estate, though, went the same way as Pruitt-Igoe, although the V&A Museum in London exhibited the carcass of a flat at the 2018 Venice Biennale, repeating Read's misunderstanding of the proper design relations between housing and everyday aesthetics.

The literal demolition of some social housing also revealed a decline in the political idea of designing, funding, and maintaining it. But, in any case, are design's aesthetic aspirations for life in estates and cities realistic? John Boughton provides many useful examples for answering this question.[95] One is the story of Hulme Crescents in Manchester, UK. The housing estate was designed as 'a solution to the problems of twentieth-century living which would be the equivalent in quality of that reached for the requirements of eighteenth-century Bloomsbury and Bath'.[96] It was designed by the architects Lewis Womersley and Hugh Wilson; work began in 1965 and was completed in 1971. The homes were designed to build a community through use of 'streets in the sky'. The scheme also included a library, communal laundry, and pool, churches, pubs, and clubs. Its design problem was conceived then, in a city council document, as creating a wholly new environment, with new communities, which would create 'fuller and happier lives for the people of Manchester'.[97] Soon though the lived experience of the estate proved otherwise. Many problems were technical, caused by serious structural issues associated with poor design. But while they could be solved, the everyday experience of living in Hulme did not accord with administrators' and designers' plans and hopes: 'its open spaces remained formless and bleak; that pedestrian-friendly diversion of traffic enclosed and isolated it within two large dual carriageways. The street life and buzz . . . were absent'.[98] Additionally, 'communal routes intended to foster community . . . provided "rat runs". . . for those whose intentions were far from friendly'.[99] It was demolished in the early 1990s. Political arguments developed, as they were at the same time with Pruitt-Igoe in America, that large-scale public housing estates only encouraged and facilitated criminality. Like Pruitt-Igoe, many socio-economic factors were involved in its failure.

But the issue for aesthetic functionalism about design at a community level is one about the extent to which 'fuller and happier' lives on estates and in urban areas can be designed at all. Doubt is thrown on this extended aim of the design apology by examples outside of large social housing estates. Estates built on Howard's garden-city model also reveal a root cause of any failure to effectively design a community. Hampstead Garden Suburb in London (1906–) was built on an idealized model of the home, albeit radically different from that at Hulme and similar estates. Its founder, Henrietta Barnett, also shared general social-reforming goals with Manchester's local government. But a report on the estate in the 1970s by a 'Design Study Group' noted that 'the idealised medieval country cottage which so influenced the Arts and Crafts movement and the architecture and thinking in Garden City planning' soon became 'unfit to live in'.[100] The report has a telling summary: 'the problem today – changing needs'.[101] And so: 'Quite naturally the new resident wants to modernise his house, to repair it, to discard the useless and obsolete and adapt the house to the needs of his family.'[102] The study concluded that its most important lesson learned was about 'the problem of integrating new residents into the Suburb'.[103] The Suburb had rules for residents, parodied in this satirical rhyme: 'O Welcome to the Suburb/ A green and pleasant land, Where everything you want to do/ Is certain to be banned'.[104]

Perhaps the Case Study House programme in the United States adopted a more realistic approach to the utopian aspirations of designing communities and better everyday experiential lives. It was started by *Arts & Architecture* magazine in 1945 in Los Angeles.[105] Motivated by the problem of US post-war housing needs as a design problem, its approach was practical and pragmatic, arguing for designers to 'get down to some cases' rather than just writing opinion pieces. 'Case Study Houses' included the Eameses' prototype noted in Chapter 5. But while the Eames House evoked a personal home concept, mass housing and community life was still the goal of these designs. And on familiar design apology grounds, the magazine chose designers for their 'obvious talents', with their 'ability to evaluate realistically housing in terms of need … and create "good" living conditions' in mind.[106] While the Case Study House programme is another example of the design apology in its aspirations for designing the good life, it nevertheless duly noted that 'the whole matter is surrounded by conditions over which few of us have any control'.[107] Evidence suggests that these 'conditions' include socio-economic ones of course, like public funding, changing demographics, and poverty. But also, that 'good' – put in scare quotes by the organizers of the Case Study Houses project – in the context of designing communities has two key meanings for design work: (a) good design meets needs, but needs change with changing technologies and peoples' expectations; and (b) in meeting needs, good design creates everyday living conditions but cannot create, although perhaps it can encourage, everyday aesthetic lives.

Awareness in the professional design world of the complexity of good design at a community level is evident in, for example, an issue of the *Harvard Design Magazine* called simply 'America'. So, it is understood that socio-economic contexts help set parameters of design problems: for example, the commissioner of the Department of Planning and Development in Chicago talks of the 'need for American architecture to operate with a deeper agenda, and for architects to also be embedded in the social, economic, environmental, and political decision-making that lead them to commissions'.[108] Also, it is understood that urban design should be 'fundamentally integrated' with thinking about the economic challenge of affordable mass housing against the American dream of single-family dwellings.[109] But the design problem that is addressed by 'America' stretches the design apology to its full: 'It's time to reexamine the prevailing notion of America as a concept, as a culture, as a country, and as a state of mind.'[110] Designing communities in that intellectual context while also engaging decision-making involving social, economic, political, and environmental concerns invites the simpler, more fundamental question of concern for the design apology: can urban areas be designed to change everyday lives aesthetically as well as functionally?

Smart, happy cities

Antonio Sant'Elia did not plan a city or even a building in functional detail, but his new city building drawings, with their traffic lanes, railways, viaducts, and bridges, have given the 'city of the future' an

Figure 10 La Citta Nuova building, Antonio Sant'Elia, 1914. Abbus Acastra / Alamy Stock Photo.

imaginative look that persists (Fig. 10).[111] They illustrated architectural ideas proclaimed in his 1914 *Manifesto of Futurist Architecture*: a focus on 'dynamic', 'oblique and elliptical lines', combatting the predominance of 'perpendicular and horizontal lines', so that it was not 'an arid combination of practicality and usefulness, but remains art'.[112] But additionally, as reflecting ideas, never clearly expressed or explained, about the life of modern, urban man, saying for example that cities should be 'the immediate and faithful projection of ourselves'.[113] There is a supposed symbiosis of the 'the new beauty of cement and iron' with 'our state of mind is new'.[114]

While Sant'Elia's futurism is startling but crass, the first part of the twentieth century did see some designers conceiving the design problems of urban life with due complexity and sensitivity, understanding this to be a prerequisite for good design solutions for housing and cities. Elizabeth Denby, for example, addressed the chief questions for 'an intelligent plan of development or redevelopment'.[115] Denby offers a critical view of the garden-city interpretation of the good life. Their 'solutions strike at the heart of compact, orderly, intellectually stimulating urban life, sacrificing as they do the positive gains of companionship to the negative ones of segregation, isolation and loneliness'.[116] She also predicted that a vast fringe of new housing might be built that left the core of the town standing empty and rotting. She concluded that

> the mass of evidence shows that the British housing problem has been cruelly over-simplified. Good housing is not the absence of slums any more than good health is just the absence of disease. Slum clearance in Britain is not merely a question of substituting a dirty box for a clean one. It is not a problem which can be solved by better plumbing.[117]

Denby therefore suggested that the complexity of the design problem of urban living be recognized by employing a variety of experts and by engaging people in existing cities. So: 'a small commission consisting of, say, an economist, an engineer, an architect, a town-planner, a doctor, a sociologist, an artist and an administrator', 'discussing local problems with local people, advising both the officials and the general public'.[118] 'The needs of Glasgow, Wigan, Durham and Newlyn are too different to be met by the application of the same official standards.'[119]

Denby's views reflect design's attempts to square the circle of quick slum clearance and rebuilding communities. And, additionally, expressive of the hopes for UK New Towns, new communities and towns were to be 'more efficient, more healthy and more beautiful' than what stood before.[120] Into the mix of the early and mid-twentieth design problem, Frank Pick added both thoughts about the inherited value of cities and city-planning's aim of generating social and civic values.[121] Focused on London, he noted its great variety and that it is 'typical of the best city life at this stage of evolution'; but added that 'it is certain that the future of London cannot be an accident like the past. If it is to hold together, to remain a workable, manageable unit, it must now be planned, be designed, be organised.'[122] Similarly, Ralph Tubbs's potted history of cities and the challenge of the twentieth century is illustrated by the front cover of his *Living in Cities*: four images are used to illustrate 'Long Ago' (a city dominated by a cathedral); 'Yesterday' (an industrial cityscape of tenements and billowing, polluting smoke from factory chimneys); 'To-day' (a bombed, destroyed city); and 'To-Morrow?' (a designer's hands with set square and pencil at a draughtsman's board).[123] They represent a beautiful but anachronistic past; an unplanned, unsound, industrial heritage; a ruinous present; a clear, clean, designed future. The twenty-first-century design problem for urban areas might simply substitute the ecological problems of 'To-day' and the technologies now available to designers for 'To-Morrow'. Tubbs, like Denby, perhaps prefigures the design work now aimed at smart, happy cities when he conceives the town as a living organism planned for home, work, education, health, and recreation.[124] And that, given that conception, a range of design expertise is required.

The concept of the 'smart' city is centred on energy consumption. But alongside is a 'social living' component. In the design world, urban design projects combining these two components – ecological and social – are called 'smart'. I want to briefly indicate how these twin concerns might align with aesthetic functionalism about design. Clearly, the ecological component of smart city design is primarily a functional requirement put on buildings and urban quarters to use renewable energies, cut down on traffic pollution and noise, and drastically reduce energy consumption. To stop suburban sprawl, the design problem also engages the need to re-densify cities by regenerating old, industrial areas. While the former set of problems are addressed technologically, building new homes and amenities in 'downtown' or 'inner city' areas presents social problems. Combining the ecological and the social, smart design must acknowledge that while the technological future can be managed, the social future cannot. Designers put in place buildings and living conditions which they assess will result in harmonious living. But only time and future experience and observation will tell if this is so. Still, a US government-sponsored competition for green homes, for example, has run for several years and does engage tests for the everyday practical demands of living.[125] Tests of neighbourliness might be impossible, but smart designers make claims for design elements that add 'social capital' to their urban projects. So, while some smartly designed urban areas might look inspired by futurist architecture, their aesthetic design impulse is not Sant'Elia's – the artful, sci-fi city of the future, representing the 'new man' – but an everyday experiential aesthetics of urban life.

The 'social living' component of smart design of urban areas relates, too, to the idea of designing a 'happy city'. The idea of the 'happy city' has been recently (re)proposed by Charles Montgomery.[126] The city has always been a happiness project, he argues, tracing it back to debates about the good life in Greek city-state Athens and Aristotle's conception of *eudaimonia*.[127] Arguing on the basis that people's happiness rests on shared ideas about real needs and desires, Montgomery lists these as aims of the happy city: promoting joy, health, freedom, resilience, fairness, friendship, and a sense of common fate.[128] He believes these are affected by the 'sprawlscape' of many cities.[129]

Montgomery's account of 'happy' seems only to echo the intentions of many urban design projects. In one respect also they all share an idea about the aesthetic effect on happiness of visual ugliness: of urban spawl, for example. In this, it is worth attending to Ian Nairn's view of Subtopia again. But this time to analyse how it suggests aesthetic functionalism about urban planning. Nairn thought that the central task for designers was to counter Subtopian planning, the kind that makes one type of scenery standard. What had to be done was 'to maintain and intensify the difference between places'.[130] That was 'the basic principle of visual planning'.[131] Nairn's aesthetic experience of places is visual and mobile, an aesthetic functionalism about design that is clear when he states that aesthetic experience is the end to which 'sociology, traffic circulation, industry, housing hygiene – are means'.[132] It bears reiterating because it is a bold aesthetic claim about how we plan our environment: that the test of planning is aesthetic. Nairn understands that social lives, mobility, work, and health present fundamental needs for designers to meet.[133] But if they are met at the cost of destroying the visual environment, of our lived everyday experience of our environs, then they deny us the end to which they were designed to be means. It follows that we must have the capacity to aesthetically experience the world so that we can make demands for good design. In Nairn's terms we need 'to be able to see and feel'.[134] I suggest, also, then that this resonates with Kenya Hara's ideas about aesthetic education for good design, that without aesthetically sophisticated desires, we get the places we deserve.[135]

Conclusion

The most far-reaching aspiration of the design apology, for designing whole communities and their everyday aesthetic lives, is only truly meaningful if it drives real urban design problems and solutions. But it seems unlikely that the needs of human flourishing associated with social living can be delineated sufficiently for design solutions to be tested with the same rigour as products of everyday use. The more precise aesthetics of product design – things that can be fully tested with users – contrasts with the more circumspect aesthetics of designing lives and communities. Examples from garden cities, new towns, and other design-led urban projects bear that doubt and contrast out. For example, from the early twentieth century, the modernist design idiom of the 'New Flat' and related 'radically new ways of living' might seem to have closely delineated the design problem for urban living, but the cost was often unliveable social housing projects. In any case, such notions of 'home' and 'ways of living' properly reflect a variety of norms and cultures, and so a range of design solutions. Even then, any number of sociologists, social psychologists, economists, and scientists might be engaged in designing mass housing and urban areas, but still, designing 'happiness' is a bridge too far. Yet meeting a city's functional requirements in ways that do not discourage human vitality and aesthetic experiential value in everyday city life are still legitimately an interest of, and should drive, good design.

Conclusion

The problem of design revisited

An ambivalence runs through design in its wastefulness and yet ambitions for cleanliness and efficiency. Designers work in economies determined on growth; but they hanker after sustainability. Designers want to create, and we desire new things; but what are our real needs and how do we flourish? Dieter Rams's resolution is contained in his 'less, but better' motto. Moreover, he has focused design work on a set of 'less and less' tasks. So, where Deyan Sudjic described the problem of design around different facets of 'waste' – not simply over-production, but objects of little value and wasted lives consuming them – Rams assigns designers this work: 'less and less' 'products whose production and use squander resources', 'products that stimulate the desire to buy', 'products that are nothing more than fashion', 'products that break quickly, wear out and age prematurely'.[1]

Rams's 'less and less' tasks therefore revisit the problem of design and the principles of good design he established fifty years before. For product design at least, they go beyond a singular ecological drive, although there is little doubt that the publicity of climate change is central in driving 'less and less' thinking about design. But Rams is also effectively arguing that designers should *determine* what kind and range of products are properly desirable. In that, he shares Sudjic's broad 'waste' view of the problem of design and endorses Kenya Hara's task for design – that it educates our desires and tastes in things. I have argued too that the design apology extends to the design of communities and that the notion of the 'smart city' chimes with

Rams's 'less and less' tasks for products. Some of these issues only confirm the problem of design from the outset, given its mass production, especially ideas relating to Packard's account of deliberate obsolescence and its relation to commercial marketing and national demands for economic growth. Still, ideas about stimulated good and bad desires for products, and so about 'kinds of products' and 'fashions' that are problematic for ideas about the quality of our experiential lives with things, should be of particular interest to philosophical aesthetics. The problem of design sets questions that properly demand an aesthetic context and benchmark: what is it like to use well-designed things? to have them around? to live in designed homes and cities?

Justin McGuirk identifies a new generation of designers more aware of the social and environmental contexts of good design beyond the product itself.[2] But I have noted that awareness of the problem of design in those contexts is not new to design but a feature of its existence. So, can designers be relied on to resist 'sales and marketing' and rather set good design in aesthetic contexts? For that, I argue that the design apology effectively sets the problem of design in the context of the philosophical aesthetics of need, experience, and value. Its aesthetic functionalism about design endorses and deepens a developmental understanding of the role of the aesthetic in our everyday lives. It shows how good design is an integral part of the concept of good living. Concerned with need, experience, and value but not with *telos* ('ultimate ends'), designers, still, freely pursue the possible ends of humankind.

The interior design magazine *Dwell* ran a survey of readers, published in its September/October 2021 issue, asking 'what issues should emerging designers be concerned with?'[3] This a sample of the answers: 'how to cope with climate change'; 'sustainability and affordability'; 'affordable housing'; 'nontoxic materials for everything'; 'building codes that incorporate building science'; 'giving voice and opportunity to a diverse community'; 'simplicity not the latest gadget'; 'incorporating innovative, new, and locally sourced materials into products and designs'; and so on. They mainly reflect current concerns, that is, social and environmental concerns. It is, of course, a random survey and an unknown audience. Still, philosophically, there is nothing here to counter, and indeed such answers confirm, the core idea of aesthetic functionalism that good design is stable around the concepts of need, function, and experience; and that these concepts play out in practical terms around use, affordability, technology and materials, and the built and natural environment. For designers, a FUTURES exhibition at the Smithsonian Institute in 2022 similarly revealed current concerns but within the recognizable design apology.[4] Like a 2018 exhibition at the Design Museum in London called 'The Future Starts Here', it showcased objects as 'a landscape of possibilities for the near future': 'wearable technology and smartphone appliances … projects that introduced unconventional ways of practicing politics, designs for internet connectivity, space travel, and concepts about living forever'.[5] Reflecting on these exhibitions, Zara Arshad wondered 'whose future?' was being designed. Arshad rightly observes that both exhibitions revealed possibilities and were not prescriptive about future societies. But the design apology asserts that design does have goals; and analysis reveals they are meaningfully tested against general criteria, albeit with cultural variations, related to human needs, function, and flourishing. The question of 'whose future?' sets a permanent context for further inquiry for the philosophy of need and everyday aesthetics.

Future inquiry, designing ourselves

To reiterate, revisiting the problem of design in the light of analysis of the design apology establishes that the real problem of design is identifying needs associated with human flourishing. In that practical work, designers provide real solutions not just to our wants but to our real needs, and in doing so they enrich our understanding of the idea of need too. In other words, the relationship between design work and the philosophy of need can be one that is valuable to both. Also, 'less and less' for design work is not understood as merely an ecological imperative but an experiential one. I believe this should focus enquiry in the everyday aesthetics paradigm on design work. It also feeds into ideas about aesthetic education for everyday life.

Design work has long taken humanity beyond basic needs associated with survival. Beyond survival to creating what we want to be as a species; design therefore is about 'designing ourselves'. The design apology properly asks questions about what is good for the development of human capabilities, imagination, and experience. It should ask now, for example, whether there is too much smart technology in our lives; too many needs too easily met, even. In that sense, the sustainability issue current in design thinking and work, is one about sustaining recognizably human life, not just the planet. David Pye noted the aesthetic importance of well-made things, suggesting good design is 'clear evidence of competence and assurance, and it is an ingredient of civilization to be continually faced with that evidence'.[6] This is perhaps a desire for good design that needs to be educated, given that designs are so often marketed for their ease and convenience, and so that we reject the ubiquity of 'just-one-click' designs. But this only follows from understanding the concept of need in terms of flourishing and enrichment.

In the science fiction play R.U.R., the general manager of the company mass producing robots argues that their manufacture was driven by wanting to 'turn the whole of mankind into the aristocracy of the world. An aristocracy nourished by millions of mechanical slaves. Unrestricted, free, and perfect men.'[7] Moreover, 'it was not an evil dream, to shatter the servitude of labour. Of the dreadful and humiliating labour that man had to undergo. The unclean and murderous drudgery… work was too hard, life was too hard.'[8] But R.U.R.'s psychologist-in-chief finally wonders, as the robots inevitably take over, rather than the clean, labour-free world, what happened to 'Enjoyment. Lovely Things.'[9] The trajectory of design history might seem analogous.

In wanting to improve everyday lives, human beings turned to designing labour-saving devices, to ideas about cleanliness, ease, speed, and convenience. Indeed, Herbert Read wondered about the possibility of the 'redemption of the robot' but only in so far as it released human potential and aesthetic lives.[10] Perhaps, after all, that is the design apology in essence; its aesthetic functionalism concerned both with our easeful functioning and our aesthetic development. If so, the 'danger of the robot' remains for design. For example, if virtual worlds are not fundamentally opposed to reality but are part of an emerging 'Reality+', then designers of these worlds face the same fundamental philosophical issues of meeting real+ needs and what that means still in terms of human flourishing.[11] David Chalmers warns how the control big tech has over the virtual aspects of our everyday lives impacts free will and personal identity. It potentially diminishes real choice and subverts the development of true selfhood. But so have all our technologies when not of our making. 'Wage slaves', 'robot/digital slaves', the problem and solution is the same for design: understanding the design apology in aesthetic terms, with good designs working as tools enabling aesthetic experience and value in our everyday lives.

In that context it is notable that Rams ends his foreword to a catalogue of his complete design works to the present day by quoting the philosopher Karl Popper: 'since we can never know anything for sure, it is simply not worth searching for certainty; but it is well worth searching for truth; and we do this chiefly by searching for mistakes, so that we can correct them.'[12] Popper famously contrasted the 'open society' where actions are freely assessed and monitored, criticized through debate, and change happens in a piecemeal fashion, with authoritarian 'closed' ones. No doubt Rams uses the quote to indicate the dangers of 'closed' thinking in design work. Perhaps he had in mind Le Corbusier's demands for 'platonic grandeur, mathematical order'.[13] Good design has its aims, but they are experiential and tested against the quality of our everyday aesthetic lives rather than some abstract or political order.

I conclude then with an example of a designed, aesthetic life. Ian Nairn quotes Harold John Massingham's *Through the Wilderness* in 'a short anthology of the philosophical background to Subtopia'.[14] For Nairn, it records the fulfilment of Subtopia in a part of the UK where Massingham is also designing and building his own home. Nairn uses quotes that rail against the absence of difference between one town and village and another. But Massingham's account is also positive about his own house-building, which is both real and a metaphor for the 'the cooperation of man with nature': 'it is the aim of this book to illustrate their partnership . . . far and near, and to suggest that it is the way of peace'.[15] Through accounts of his own design decisions about his house and its garden, Massingham suggests that he can 'build a new house with the inventions, facilities and technique of my own period which would attach itself to the landscape as unerringly as any old familiar of thatch and mullion and eave'.[16] The 'peaceful' design solution is one in which not only are the views from it pleasant but that, however new the building, 'its surroundings found it seemly to them' too.[17]

Le Corbusier loved the airplane because, in his terms, the design problem of the 'plane was set out functionally and thus properly solved: a 'machine for flying', an engineering problem of suspension and propulsion, not some metaphorical wish to fly like a bird. In Rex Warner's allegorical novel, *The Aerodrome*, though, the life of an airman is too purely functional for the protagonist: '"That the world be clean": I remembered my father's words. Clean indeed it was and most intricate, fiercer than tigers, wonderful and infinitely forgiving.'[18] In that worldview, perhaps, lies a sense of the fully human context of good design's aims and its essentially functional and aesthetic, experiential character, and value.

Notes

Introduction

1 Aristotle, *The Nicomachean Ethics*, trans. J. A. K. Thomson (London: Penguin Books, 2004), 4.
2 Deyan Sudjic, *The Language of Things* (London: Penguin Books, 2008), 8.
3 Ibid., 5.
4 Milan Semelak, 'Stop Making the World a Worse Place', *Backstage Talks: Dialogues on Design and Business*, 5, 2020, 140.
5 Ibid., 140.
6 Rachel Garrahan, 'The Watch That Saved Cartier', *Vogue*, May 2021, 118.
7 Justin McGuirk, 'Introduction,' in *Waste Age*, ed. Design Museum (London: Design Museum, 2021), 7.
8 Design Council, 'Our Mission', accessed 29 July 2022.
9 Ibid.
10 Vance Packard, *The Waste Makers* (London: Longmans, 1961), 5.
11 Ibid., 5.
12 Ibid., 55.
13 Ian Nairn, *Outrage* (London: The Architectural Press, 1956), unpaginated 'Contents' page.
14 Ibid., 370.
15 Kenya Hara, *Designing Japan: A Future Built on Aesthetics*, trans. Maggie Kinser and Yukiko Naito (Zurich: Lars Muller, 2018), 80.
16 Ibid., 80.
17 McGuirk, 'Introduction,' in Design Museum, *Waste Age*, 9.
18 William Francis Forbes Sempill, 'Foreword,' in *Design*, ed. Anthony Bertram (London: Penguin Books, 1938), vii.
19 Ibid., vii.
20 Ibid., vii.
21 Gareth Williams, *Design: An Essential Introduction* (London: Design Museum, 2015), 8.

22 Dieter Rams's '10 Principles of Good Design' are ubiquitous in the design world and available at many online sources. See, for example, Design Museum, 'What Is "Good" Design? A Quick Look at Dieter Rams' Ten Principles,' accessed 29 July 2022.

23 Ibid.

24 See Bibliography for details.

25 Deyan Sudjic, 'Introduction', in *Beazley Designs of the Year 2019* (London: Design Museum, 2019), 9.

26 Ibid., 9.

27 See, for example, the editorial to the Autumn 2020 issue of *Disegno: The Quarterly Journal of Design*.

28 Emily King, 'Where Were We?', in *Beazley Designs of the Year 2020*, ed. Emily King (London: Design Museum, 2020), 15.

29 See, for example, the Dasgupta Review on the Economics of Biodiversity in 2020. Its analysis echoed the earlier similar Stern Review on the Economics of Climate Change in 2006.

30 Zuzana Kvetkova, 'Editorial', *Backstage Talks: Designers on Design and Business* 5, 2020.

31 The approach is akin then to Monroe Beardsley's for artworks when he argued that there would be no aesthetics if everyone was silent about works of art: *Aesthetics* (Indianapolis, IN: Hackett, 1981), 1.

Chapter 1

1 Janet McCracken, 'Book Reviews', *Journal of Aesthetics and Art Criticism* 58, no. 1 (2000): 76–79.

2 Ibid., 76.

3 Ibid., 77.

4 Ibid., 79.

5 Jonathan Bean, 'Review of *Routledge Companion to Design Studies* (2016)', *Journal of Design History* 30, no. 2 (May 2017): 243.

6 Ibid., 243.

7 McCracken, 'Book Reviews', 79, discussing Albert Borgmann's contribution to *Discovering Design: Explorations in Design Studies*,

ed. Richard Buchanan and Victor Margolin (Chicago: University of Chicago Press, 1995).

8 Albert Borgmann, 'The Depth of Design', in *Design Philosophy Reader*, ed. Anne-Marie Willis (London: Bloomsbury, 2019), 22.

9 Ibid., 22.

10 Ibid., 24.

11 Ibid., 23.

12 Ibid., 23.

13 Ibid., 23.

14 Ibid., 23.

15 Ibid., 25.

16 Ibid., 25.

17 Ibid., 23.

18 Ibid., 23.

19 McCracken, 'Book Reviews', 79.

20 It should be noted that I provide a full justification for this list of core concerns and concepts in constructing the 'design apology' in Chapter 2.

21 Anne-Marie Willis, 'Introduction,' in *The Design Philosophy Reader*, ed. Anne-Marie Willis (London: Bloomsbury, 2019), 1.

22 Ibid., 3.

23 Ibid., 3.

24 Ibid., 5.

25 D. J. Huppatz, *Design: The Key Concepts* (London: Bloomsbury Visual Arts, 2019), 2.

26 Ibid., 2.

27 Ibid., 2.

28 Huppatz, *Design*, Preface.

29 See, for example, Andy Hamilton, 'The Aesthetics of Design', in *Fashion and Philosophy*, ed. Jeanette Kennett and Jessica Wolfendale (London: Blackwell, 2011) for an 'engineering versus fashion' clash involving James Dyson on the 'side' of engineering.

30 Glenn Parsons, *The Philosophy of Design* (Cambridge: Polity Press, 2016), 1.

31 That there is an existing 'philosophy of design' available for construction from the history of design and up to present-day thinking about design

work in general is the subject of Chapter 2, especially the section 'The design apology'. 'Design and the idea of everyday aesthetics' is also examined in Chapter 3.

32 Parsons, *Philosophy of Design*, 3.
33 Ibid., 11.
34 Ibid., 68.
35 Ibid., 84.
36 Florence de Dampierre, *Chairs: A History* (New York: Harry N. Abrams, 2006).
37 Parsons, *Philosophy of Design*, 103.
38 Ibid., 111.
39 Ibid., 129.
40 Darren Bradley, 'Yesterday's Vision of Tomorrow', *The Modernist* 33 (December 2019): 12.
41 But I do have more to say on modernism's utopian aspirations as representative of a fundamental feature of design work in Chapter 6.
42 Jane Forsey, *The Aesthetics of Design* (Oxford: Oxford University Press, 2013), 6.
43 Kant quoted in Forsey, *Aesthetics of Design*, 141.
44 Forsey, *Aesthetics of Design*, 181.
45 I will say more on this firstly in the context of constructing the 'design apology' from what designers say about their work; and secondly when examining product designs.
46 Forsey, *Aesthetics of Design*, 187. Designers and design critics prioritize how things work rather than their look; and that suggests an educative role too. So, for example, a design critic reacts, like Forsey, to a companion's falsely positive judgement of a sugar pot: 'look at this mechanism . . . over-engineered trash. Too many parts that could go wrong. My companion frowned. That's the bit I like about it, they explained. It's fun'. The design critic's view is that the sugar pot is properly not about fun but the 'business of administering coffee'. Oli Stratford, 'The Sugar Pot', *Disegno: The Quarterly Journal of Design* 31 (Winter 2021): 3–4.
47 Forsey argues the latter about the programme of the Everyday Aesthetics movement, which is the topic of Chapter 3.

48 Roger Scruton, 'A Bit of Help from Wittgenstein', *British Journal of Aesthetics* 51, no. 3 (July 2011): 309–19.
49 David Pye, *The Nature of Design* (London: Studio Vista, 1964), 10.
50 Ibid., 83.
51 Ibid., 83.
52 Ibid., 96.
53 Ibid., 96.
54 Ibid., 84.
55 Ibid., 91.
56 Ludwig Wittgenstein, *Lectures & Conversations on Aesthetics, Psychology and Religious Belief*, ed. Cyril Barrett (Oxford: Blackwell, 1966), 3.
57 Ibid., 13. Wittgenstein's theoretic example reflects his own practical interest, given his involvement in the design of 'Haus Wittgenstein' in Vienna in the 1920s. And the design of entrance doors is a matter for international design contests and attests to the depth of design: see www.doorscape.eu (accessed 1 September 2022), for example, for the idea of the entrance as 'a valuable design area' concerned with 'the access to a place for domestic use in its multiple meanings: cultural, functional, and formal'.
58 Wittgenstein, *Lectures & Conversations on Aesthetics,* 5.
59 Ibid., 5.
60 Ibid., 13.
61 Roger Scruton, 'Bit of Help from Wittgenstein', 309.
62 Ibid., 310.
63 Ibid., 310.
64 Ibid., 310.
65 Ibid., 311.
66 Andy Hamilton, 'The Anatomy of Architecture', in *Scruton's Aesthetics*, ed. Andy Hamilton and Nick Zangwill (London: Palgrave Macmillan, 2012), 184.
67 Ibid., 184.
68 Ibid., 180.
69 Ibid., 184.
70 Ibid., 184.
71 See Chapter 2's section entitled 'The design apology'.

72 Scruton, 'Bit of Help from Wittgenstein', 319.
73 This evidence is provided in Part II, where I examine products, homes, and cities in relation to aesthetic functionalism about design.
74 Edward Winters, 'Against Neatness, and the Neateners Who Would Neaten Us', in Hamilton and Zangwill, *Scruton's Aesthetics*.
75 Ibid., 213.
76 Ibid., 230.
77 Ian Nairn, *Nairn's London* (London: Penguin Books, 2014). I have in mind his descriptions of Pelham Crescent in Kensington and Hide Tower in Pimlico, but he provides many more similar examples.
78 'A Matter of Definitions', Editorial, *Disegno: The Quarterly Journal of Design* 15 (2017): 7–8. I could add, think also of the myriad design-related quasi-theoretic magazines and journals on design and its specialisms. Any internet search or visit to a design museum or gallery will attest to that.
79 Ibid., 8.

Chapter 2

1 Design Council, 'Our Mission: Purpose, Vision and Values', accessed 29 July 2022.
2 Design Council, 'Our Work', accessed 29 July 2022.
3 Ibid.
4 Design Council, 'What Is Design?', accessed 29 July 2022.
5 Design Museum, *Designs of the Year* (London: Design Museum, 2016).
6 "About," IDEA Center, accessed 1 July 2022.
7 Catherine Ince, ed., *The World of Charles and Ray Eames* (London: Thames & Hudson, 2015), 256. Transcript of a film interview conducted with Charles and Ray Eames by Madame L. Amic in 1972 titled *Design Q&A*.
8 Ibid., 256.
9 Ibid., 256.
10 Ibid., 138. Uncredited introductory text to 'The Art of Living' section of Ince, *World of Charles and Ray Eames*.

11 Ibid., 138. Charles Eames quoted from a *Time* article, 'Sympathetic Seat', 10 July 1950, 45–46.

12 Anthony Bertram, *Design in Everyday Things* (London: British Broadcasting Corporation, 1937), 1.

13 Ibid., 1.

14 Anna Sandberg Falk, 'Sponsor's Foreword,' in *Home Futures*, ed. Eszter Steierhoffer, Justin McGuirk, and Design Museum (London: Design Museum, 2018), 5.

15 Ibid., 5.

16 Ince, *World of Charles and Ray Eames*, 256.

17 Ibid., 16.

18 Henry Dreyfuss, *Designing for People* (New York: Simon and Schuster, 1955), frontispiece.

19 Raymond Loewy, *Industrial Design* (London: Fourth Estate, 1988), 47.

20 Raymond Loewy, *Never Leave Well Enough Alone* (New York: Simon and Schuster, 1951), 83. Loewy was the first designer to be the cover story of *Time* magazine on 3 October 1949.

21 Loewy, *Industrial Design*, 18.

22 Ibid., 36.

23 Ibid., 36.

24 Ibid., 8.

25 Ibid., 8.

26 Ibid., 15.

27 Rams, '10 Principles', in Design Museum, 'What Is "Good" Design? A Quick Look at Dieter Rams' Ten Principles'.

28 Ibid.

29 Ibid.

30 Ibid.

31 Dieter Rams, 'Foreword,' in *Dieter Rams: The Complete Works*, ed. Klaus Kemp (London: Phaidon, 2020), 7.

32 Ibid., 7.

33 Rams quoted by Kemp, *Dieter Rams*, 9.

34 Ibid.

35 Ibid.

36 Ibid.

37 Rams, '10 Principles' in Design Museum, 'What Is "Good" Design? A Quick Look at Dieter Rams' Ten Principles'.
38 Rams, 'Foreword,' in Kemp, *Dieter Rams*, 6.
39 Ibid., 7.
40 Ibid., 7.
41 Ibid., 7.
42 Charlotte Perriand, 'Wood or Metal?', in *Charlotte Perriand: An Art of Living*, ed. Mary McLeod (New York: Harry N. Abrams, 2003), 251.
43 Ibid., 251.
44 Ibid., 253.
45 Mary McLeod, 'Charlotte Perriand's *Art de Vivre*', in McLeod, *Charlotte Perriand*, 10.
46 Ibid., 10.
47 Charlotte Perriand, 'The Family Dwelling: Its Economic and Social Development', in McLeod, *Charlotte Perriand*, 255.
48 In the 1920s Le Corbusier's specifications for the modern home included that we 'demand a vacuum cleaner'. See Le Corbusier, *Towards a New Architecture*, trans. Frederick Etchells (London: The Architectural Press, 1946), 115.
49 Charlotte Perriand, 'The Art of Dwelling', in McLeod, *Charlotte Perriand*, 262.
50 Ibid., 262.
51 Ibid., 262.
52 Justin McGuirk, 'Introduction,' in *Charlotte Perriand: The Modern Life*, ed. Design Museum (London: Design Museum, 2021), 7.
53 Charlotte Perriand quoted in McGuirk, *Charlotte Perriand*, 9. I examine Morris's everyday aesthetics in detail in Chapter 3.
54 Naomi Pollock, *Japanese Design: A Complete Sourcebook* (London: Thames & Hudson, 2020), 32. Hara's ideas follow those of Soetsu Yanagi in his 1926 'The Beauty of Miscellaneous Things' and other essays collected in *The Beauty of Everyday Things* (London: Penguin Classics, 2018), 27–58.
55 Pollock, *Japanese Design*, 32. They are not specified, although Yanagi and, more profoundly, Zen Buddhism come to mind.
56 Hara, *Designing Japan*, vii.

57 Ibid., ix.

58 Ibid., x.

59 Ibid., x.

60 Although, of course, Hara is indebted to other thinkers. His ideas echo Soetsu Yanagi's, when Yanagi claims that 'the litmus test of a country's cultural level should be the lives led by ordinary people. This level is most apparent in the utilitarian objects used on a daily basis.' Soetsu Yanagi, 'The Japan Folk Arts Museum', in *The Beauty of Everyday Things*, ed. Soetsu Yanagi (London: Penguin Classics, [1947] 2018), 325–46, 345.

61 Hara, *Designing Japan*, vii.

62 Quote on cover of *Harvard Design Magazine* No. 48, 'America', 2021, Published by the Harvard University Graduate School of Design.

63 See Design Age Institute, 'Designing for Age, Agency & Joy', accessed 31 August 2022.

64 Jeremy Myerson, 'Sometimes Frivolous, Sometimes Philosophical', *Disegno: The Quarterly Journal of Design* 29 (Summer 2021): 18–23, 18.

65 Ibid., 18.

66 David Wiggins, 'An Idea We Cannot Do Without', in *The Philosophy of Need*, ed. Soran Reader (Cambridge: Cambridge University Press, 2005), 25–50, 26.

67 Ibid., 26.

68 Ibid., 33.

69 Ibid., 33.

70 Ibid., 50.

71 I do, however, think that a 'limitation principle' is being invoked by designers who want to end design's 'waste age': as discussed in the section entitled 'The problem of design', the vital needs of the planet and human survival will surely limit our need for 'more stuff'.

72 A significant caveat to design typically not involving protecting needs is the role of design in building communities: it is discussed in Chapter 6. Anticipating the core argument there, Wiggins's example of decision-making in urban planning is apposite and relates to how design problems for mass housing and cities are best conceived. Another distinction between vital needs and needs in terms of the design

apology is the immediacy of the former. An example is someone or a group needing immediate food or shelter. The need to feed and house 'x' *now* (because they have been left homeless by some emergency, for example) is not a generalizable design problem, although designers would no doubt engage in that vital work if required. Again, however, design's role in long-term mass housing is an issue of need.

73 Andrew Belsey, 'Needs', in *The Oxford Companion to Philosophy*, ed. Ted Honderich (Oxford: Oxford University Press, 1995).
74 Alfred Edward Taylor, *Aristotle* (New York: Dover, 1955), 90.
75 Ibid., 90.
76 Philippa Foot, *Natural Goodness* (Oxford: Clarendon Press, 2001), 40.
77 Ibid., 40.
78 Soran Reader, 'Aristotle on Necessities and Needs', in Reader, *Philosophy of Need*, 135.
79 Ibid., 135.
80 Peter Kropotkin, *The Conquest of Bread* (London: Penguin Books, 2015), 100.
81 Ibid., 18.
82 Ibid., 99.
83 Ibid., 100.
84 Ibid., 100.
85 Ibid., 101.
86 Ibid., 101.
87 Ibid., 112.
88 Sudjic, *Language of Things*, 91.
89 Ibid., 91.
90 Ibid., 93.
91 Ibid., 100. If the reader needs an example, I could suggest this on the packaging of the Juicy Salif lemon squeezer designed by Philippe Starck: 'It remains unparalleled in its ability to generate discussions about its meaning and design, partly because of its unconventional use of what semiologists refer to as the decorative veil which . . . is inexorably destined to cover all objects created by man'. I return to its qualities as a lemon squeezer in Chapter 4, examining product designs in the light of the design apology.

92 Reader, 'Aristotle on Necessities', 135.
93 'Asking the Right Questions', interview with Christian Madsbjerg by Zuzana Kvetkova, *Backstage Talks: Dialogues on Design and Business* 5, 2020.
94 Ibid., 94.
95 Ibid., 94.
96 Ibid., 95.
97 Ibid., 95.
98 Ibid., 96.
99 Ibid., 97.
100 Ibid, p.97.
101 David Wiggins, *Needs, Values, Truth* (London, Blackwell, 1991), 24.
102 Ibid., 24.
103 Ibid., 39.
104 Robert Stecker, 'Aesthetic Experience and Aesthetic Value', *Philosophy Compass* 1, no. 1 (2006): 1–10, 1.
105 John Dewey, *Art as Experience* (New York: Minton, Balch & Company, 1934), 13.
106 Ibid., 13.
107 Ibid., 44.
108 For a full account of the essentially adaptive character of a Deweyan account of aesthetic experience, see Jeffrey Petts, 'Aesthetic Experience and the Revelation of Value', *Journal of Aesthetics and Art Criticism* 58, no. 1 (2000): 61–71.
109 Dewey, *Art as Experience*, 327.
110 Ibid., 326.
111 Ibid., 35.
112 Foot, *Natural Goodness*, 98.

Chapter 3

1 Crispin Sartwell, 'Aesthetics of the Everyday', in *The Oxford Handbook of Aesthetics*, ed. Jerrold Levinson (Oxford: Oxford University Press, 2003), 761.

2 Yuriko Saito, *Aesthetics of the Familiar: Everyday Life and World-Making* (Oxford: Oxford University Press, 2019).

3 I am thinking of this, for example, from Okakura Kakuzo's *The Book of Tea*: 'What Rikui [the tea-master] demanded was not cleanliness alone, but the beautiful and the natural also' (Boulder, CO: Shambhala, [1900] 2023).

4 Sartwell, 'Aesthetics of the Everyday', 763.

5 Ibid., 763.

6 Ibid., 764.

7 Ibid., 764.

8 Barbara Jones, *The Unsophisticated Arts* (London: The Architectural Press, 1951).

9 Ibid., 9.

10 Ibid., 10.

11 Yuriko Saito, *Everyday Aesthetics* (Oxford: Oxford University Press, 2007). See the section headed 'Special Experience-Based Aesthetics', 43–53, which presents the case. She takes Edward Bullough's 'disinterest' and John Dewey's 'engagement' accounts of aesthetic experience as representative of versions of it being necessarily 'special'.

12 Ibid., 43.

13 Sherri Irvin, 'The Pervasiveness of the Aesthetic in Ordinary Experience', *British Journal of Aesthetics* 48, no. 1 (2008): 29–44.

14 Ibid., 29.

15 Ibid., 30.

16 David Davies, 'Sibley and the Limits of Everyday Aesthetics', *Journal of Aesthetic Education* 49, no. 3 (Fall 2015): 50–65.

17 Christopher Dowling, 'The Aesthetics of Daily Life', *British Journal of Aesthetics* 50, no. 3 (2010): 225–42.

18 Ibid., 240.

19 Ibid., 240.

20 Ibid., 240.

21 Kevin Melchionne, 'Aesthetic Experience in Everyday Life: A Reply to Dowling', *British Journal of Aesthetics* 51, no. 4 (2011): 437–42.

22 Dewey, *Art as Experience*, 342.

23 'Art and Civilization' is the title of the last chapter of *Art as Experience*.

24 Dewey, *Art as Experience*, 342.

25 Ibid., 343.

26 Herbert Read, *Art and Industry* (London: Faber & Faber, 1934), 40. Read notes Gropius's paper is reprinted in the *Journal of the Royal Institute of British Architects*, 19 May 1934.

27 Walter Gropius quoted by Read, *Art and Industry*, 40.

28 Ibid., 40.

29 Ibid., 40.

30 Bruno Munari, *Design as Art*, trans. Patrick Creagh (London: Penguin, 2008), 27.

31 Ibid., 27.

32 Francesca Giacomelli, 'Enzo Mari Was a Universe', *Disegno: The Quarterly Journal of Design* 28 (Spring 2021): 123–36.

33 Ibid., 125.

34 Nikolaus Pevsner, *Pioneers of Modern Design: From William Morris to Walter Gropius* (London: Penguin Books, 1991).

35 Owen Hatherley, 'Back to the Red House: William Morris after Reform and Revolution', in *How I Became a Socialist* by William Morris (London: Version, 2020), 1–15, 2.

36 Ibid., 2.

37 Ibid., 2.

38 William Morris, 'How I Became a Socialist', in *William Morris: Selected Writings*, ed. George Douglas Howard Cole (London: Nonesuch Press, 1934), 655–59, 656.

39 Ibid., 657.

40 Hatherley, 'Back to the Red House', 4.

41 Florence Boos, *Socialist Aesthetics & The Shadows of Amiens* (London: William Morris Society, 2011).

42 Ibid., 15.

43 William Morris, 'The Promise of May', available online at www.marxists.org (accessed 1 June 2021).

44 Gillian Naylor, 'Morris as a Pioneer of Modern Design', in *William Morris Now*, ed. Roger Simon (London: Institute of Contemporary Arts, 1984), 81–86.

45 I look in more detail at Morris's design ideas as they relate to the home and the 'beauty of life' in Chapter 5.

46 Morris quoted in Naylor, 'Morris as a Pioneer', 86.
47 William Morris, 'A Factory as It Might Be', in Cole, *William Morris*, 654.
48 By political imperatives, I refer to fundamental political concepts like 'justice' and 'equality' and so on.
49 Sherri Irvin, 'Is Aesthetic Experience Possible?', in *Aesthetics and the Sciences of Mind*, ed. Greg Currie, Matthew Kieran, Aaron Meskin, and Jon Robson (Oxford: Oxford University Press, 2014), 37–56, 45.
50 Ibid., 47.
51 Ibid., 48.
52 Paul Guyer, 'History of Modern Aesthetics', in Levinson, *Oxford Handbook of Aesthetics*, 25–62.
53 Design Museum, *Designs of the Year* (London: Design Museum, 2017).
54 Ibid.
55 Ibid.
56 Goldsmiths Street, Norwich, UK, notably the first social housing project to win this architectural award. See www.ribaj.com (accessed 11 May 2022).
57 William Lethaby, 'Education of the Architect', in *Form in Civilization*, ed. William Lethaby (Oxford: Oxford University Press, 1922), 123 and 127.
58 William Lethaby, 'Education for Appreciation or for Production?', in Lethaby, *Form in Civilization*, 128.
59 Ibid., 128.
60 Ibid., 129.
61 Saito, *Aesthetics of the Familiar*, 225.
62 Ibid., 225.
63 Ibid., 150.
64 Ibid., 61.
65 Ibid., 150. I should add that Saito develops the idea of the supposed moral input of 'care' in good design in her *Aesthetics of Care* (London: Bloomsbury Academic, 2022).
66 Ibid., 150.
67 Ibid., 151.
68 Ibid., 151.
69 Ibid., 170.
70 Ibid., 170.

71 Ibid., 165.
72 Ibid., 167.
73 Ibid., 167.
74 Ibid., 167.
75 Ibid., 168.
76 Of course, where there is evidence of wilfully second-rate design work in public buildings and housing that knowingly puts lives at risk, then clear and obvious moral issues are raised beyond 'poor design'.
77 Quoted by Fiona MacCarthy, *Walter Gropius* (London: Faber & Faber, 2020), 262.
78 Bernard Leach, *A Potter in Japan: 1952–1954* (London: Unicorn, 2015), 58.
79 Ibid., 58.
80 Ibid., 58.
81 Hara, *Designing Japan*, vii. I note too that the need for aesthetic education in good design is linked to improvements in the natural environment and public life by Sharon Irish in the context of Indian urban planning: 'Intimacy and Monumentality in Chandigarh, North India: Le Corbusier's Capitol Complex and Nek Chand Saini's Rock Garden', *Journal of Aesthetic Education* 34, no. 2 (Summer 2004): 105–15. See Chapter 6 on 'mass housing and urban planning'.
82 Ibid., 80.

Chapter 4

1 *Objectified* (2009), [Film] Dir. Gary Hustwit (Submarine Deluxe: Streaming Video).
2 Arthur Drexler, *Charles Eames: Furniture from the Design Collection, the Museum of Modern Art, New York* (New York: The Museum of Modern Art, 1973), 3.
3 Ibid., 3.
4 Ibid., 3.
5 Dreyfuss, *Designing for People*, 14.
6 Mark Elliott and Nicholas Thomas, eds., *Gifts and Discoveries* (London: Scala, 2011), 16.

7 Ibid., 17. Note too that a recent history of design by Pat Kirkham, *History of Design* (New Haven, CT: Yale University Press, 2013) spans 1400 to the present day and includes design work from East Asia, India, the Islamic World, Africa, Europe, and the Americas. The editor's introduction, even given that breadth, regards the book's scope as arbitrary in so far as design extends back to antiquity, referring to work from the late Neolithic period. Charlotte and Peter Fiell's *The Story of Design* (London: Goodman Fiell, 2013) also starts with a chapter on prehistoric tools.

8 Neil MacGregor, *The History of the World in 100 Objects* (London: Allen Lane, 2010), 13.

9 Plato, 'Republic', in *The Collected Dialogues*, ed. Edith Hamilton and Huntingdon Cairns (Princeton, NJ: Princeton University Press, 1994), 826.

10 Reported on the Smart Design company website, accessed 11 April 2022. Watching someone struggle 'with a common vegetable peeler, [the designer] set out to make ordinary kitchen tools easier for everyone to use – adding delight in the process'. And the product is sixth on a list of the greatest one hundred designs of modern times in 2020.

11 Adolf Loos, 'Chairs', in *Ornament and Crime: Thoughts on Design and Materials*, trans. Shaun Whiteside (London: Penguin, 2019), 163–72, 163. Loos continues that sufficiency is guaranteed when the product 'is so perfect that one could not add anything to it or take anything away without adversely affecting it', 164.

12 Gottfried Semper, *Style in the Technical and Tectonic Arts; or Practical Aesthetics*, trans. Harry Francis Malgrave and Michael Robinson (Los Angeles, CA: Getty Research Institute, 2004), 468.

13 Semper, *Style*, 469.

14 Loos, 'Chairs', in Whiteside, *Ornament and Crime*, 175.

15 Ibid., 175.

16 Ibid., 177.

17 Ibid., 177.

18 Ince, *World of Charles and Ray Eames*, 138 (unattributed introductory text to section headed 'The Art of Living').

19 Ibid., 138.

20 Quote attributed to the Eameses by Eames Demetrios, 'A Contemporary Practice: The Eameses in the 1940s', in Ince, *World of Charles and Ray Eames*, 20.

21 Adolf Loos, 'Ornament and Education', in *Ornament and Crime: Selected Essays*, trans. Michael Mitchell (Riverside, CA: Ariadne Press, 1998), 185.

22 Ibid, 187.

23 Loos had a keen interest in gentlemen's tailoring and his own elegant dress code marks him as a dandy, someone who wears clothes 'wisely and well'. Like Beau Brummell, being well-dressed meant a proper aesthetic sense of quality marking ostensible differences between mere and the real thing: summed up perhaps in a typical Brummell barb, 'You call that *thing* a coat?'.

24 Loos, 'Ornament and Education', in Mitchell, *Ornament and Crime*, 187.

25 Ibid., 189.

26 Ibid., 188.

27 Anthony Bertram, *Design* (London: Pelican, 1938), 70.

28 Ibid., 71. It is interesting to note, in this regard, the observation made by Deyan Sudjic, *B Is for Bauhaus: An A–Z of the Modern World* (London: Penguin Books, 2015), when he argues that 'we decorate our possessions after they have left the factory', 346. Sudjic recognizes this as a hunger for ornamentation; it is surely one that is not properly met at the factory but is a craft-like activity that we can subsequently enjoy.

29 Bertram, *Design*, 71.

30 Bertram, *Design in Everyday Things*.

31 *South Bank Exhibition, Festival of Britain, Guide* (London: His Majesty's Stationery Office, 1951), 87.

32 See Fiell and Fiell, *Story of Design*, 353.

33 Brit Insurance, *Designs of the Year* (London: Design Museum, 2011), 176.

34 I refer to Terence Conran's home store 'Habitat' in the UK and the Swiss Vitra furniture company. I say more about them in Chapter 5 in the context of design and lifestyles.

35 Loewy, *Industrial Design*, 10.

36 Ibid., 10.

37 Ibid., 10.
38 Ibid., 13. Whether Loewy in fact did what he said as a designer is a moot point. Sudjic cites Loewy as epitomizing the designer as a heroic form-giver, giving products a new skin and no more. I return to that *general notion* later in this section on 'product designers' when considering the designer as an artist, without any inference about Loewy's work or Sudjic's view of it.
39 MOMA press release, March 1946.
40 Oli Stratford, 'Designing the Batman', *Disegno: The Quarterly Journal of Design* 32 (Spring 2022): 7–8, 7.
41 Ibid., 8.
42 Peter Kapos, 'Counterpoints', *Disegno: The Quarterly Journal of Design* 30 (Autumn 2021): 53–59, 58. If a recent case study in 'good design and the market' is needed, then it is provided by Jean Prouvé's *Fauteuil Kangourou* chair, designed in 1948, and the design company Vitra's 2022 version and marketing. See Elizabeth Glickfield, 'Futureheads', *Design Reviewed* 1, January 2023, 44–51. She notes that Prouvé is now 'considered the designer's designer', admired for 'his life-long commitment to unearthing the poetics of the then-new industrial processes' (of the early twentieth century) (ibid., 45). Glickfield describes its aesthetic and functional appeal ('elegant and elemental; and not something to be scared of sitting on'). But her focus is on its marketing in the twenty-first century. It is produced in deliberately limited numbers: 150 at first. And sold with a campaign noted for 'harnessing the internet's capacity for fuelling our sense of FOMO' (Fear of Missing Out) (ibid., 46). It is a marketing campaign in sharp contrast to the utopian aspirations set by the École de Nancy for high-quality mass production that provided the educational background at the turn of the twentieth century to Prouvé's subsequent work. See also Peter Sulzer, *Jean Prouve Complete Works, Volume 1: 1917–1933* (Basel: Birkhauser, 2009).
43 Designboom.com, 'Interview with James Irvine', 4 June 2003.
44 See section entitled 'Chairs and other things' for this chair's celebrated place in design history. For Irvine's 2009 chair, see *James Irvine*, ed. Francesca Picchi with Marialaura Rossiello Irvine (London: Phaidon, 2015), 202.

45 Designboom, 'Interview with James Irvine'.
46 Ibid.
47 Francesca Picchi, 'A Thing of Beauty Is a Joy Forever', in Picchi and Rossiello Irvine, *James Irvine*, 31.
48 Ibid., 31.
49 'Design Dance, James Irvine 07', in Picchi and Rossiello Irvine, *James Irvine*, 108; and 'Utopian Design Antibody, James Irvin, 2008', in Picchi and Rossiello Irvine, *James Irvine*, 15.
50 *Backstage Talks: Dialogues on Design and Business* 5, 56.
51 Ibid., 57.
52 Max Donnelly, *Christopher Dresser: Design Pioneer* (London: Thames & Hudson, 2021), 12.
53 Ibid., 11, quoting Dresser.
54 Ibid., 71, quoting Dresser.
55 I discuss how Dresser's 'name' and association with artistic good taste was also utilized to endorse a range of household items in Chapter 5.
56 Kees Dorst, 'But Is It Art?', in *Design and Art*, ed. Alex Coles (London: Whitechapel Gallery, 2007), 88.
57 Norman Potter, 'Is a Designer an Artist?', in Coles, *Design and Art*, 32.
58 Ibid., 32.
59 Quoted in Susie Hodge, *What Makes Great Design: 80 Masterpieces Explained* (London: Francis Lincoln, 2014), 105. And yet it should also be noted that the author, while overemphasizing the value of visual effects towards good design in the organization of the book, presents a more measured view of design work in her 'Introduction' when stating that 'designers analyze the requirements of potential users, seek dexterous solutions, and produce attractive, practical, desirable and affordable products' (ibid., 15).
60 Sudjic, *B Is for Bauhaus*, 465.
61 Ibid., 470.
62 Ibid., 464.
63 In any case, a little research can of course reveal a named designer or design team responsible for a product. The issue at stake is about how that fact has, properly, no bearing on aesthetic functionality.
64 Sudjic, *B Is for Bauhaus*, 470.

65 Eddie Opara, 'Design Is about Creating Systems, not Solving Problems', in *Backstage Talks: Dialogues on Design and Business* 5, 2020, 114.
66 Sudjic, *B Is for Bauhaus*, 76.
67 Deyan Sudjic, 'Introduction,' in *Fifty Chairs That Changed the World*, ed. Michael Czerwinski (London: Octopus, 2009), 6.
68 Czerwinski, *Fifty Chairs*, 9.
69 Le Corbusier quoted in Czerwinski, *Fifty Chairs*, 9.
70 Le Corbusier, *Towards a New Architecture*, 109.
71 Sudjic, *B Is for Bauhaus*, 78.
72 Ibid., 82.
73 Loos, 'Chairs', in Whiteside, *Ornament and Crime*, 167.
74 Max Beerbohm, *Rossetti and His Circle* (New Haven, CT: Yale University Press, 1987), unpaginated appendix.
75 Sudjic, *B Is for Bauhaus, 82*.
76 Parsons, *Philosophy of Design*, 84.
77 MOMA press release 'New Furniture Designs and Techniques Have Initial Showing at Museum of Modern Art', March 1946 (accessed from MOMA website 26 March 2021).
78 Magnus Englund, 'Bend It like Morrison', *Disegno: The Quarterly Journal of Design* 30 (Autumn 2021): 78–83, 82.
79 Ibid., 83.
80 Janet McCracken, 'Why We Love Our Phones: A Case Study in the Aesthetics of Gadgets', in *Comparative Everyday Aesthetics*, ed. Eva Kit Wah Man and Jeffrey Petts (Amsterdam: Amsterdam University Press, 2023). The appeal of simply *having and using* new gadgets precedes mobile phones it seems, given the example of Karel Capek's love of his 'new invention', a Swedish vacuum cleaner, in the 1920s: '[I] call up the whole house to come and have a look at how much dust there is in the little bag. I can assure you that the amazement of the assembled throng is the chief delight in cultivating a vacuum cleaner, and that it provides you with priceless satisfaction every day': 'An Invention' in *Believe in People: The Essential Karel Capek,* trans. Sarka Tobrmanova-Kuhnova (London: Faber & Faber, 2010), 142–44, 143. Perhaps the phenomenon he and McCracken describe is related to FOMO as well as the 'fun' of new gadgets.

81 Dreyfuss, *Designing for People*, 26.

82 Ibid., 27.

83 Descriptions of some of the products nominated for 2019 and 2020 UK Designs of the Year awards.

84 The phrase circulates in Arts and Crafts literature without attribution; perhaps William Lethaby coined the phrase in a lecture later published in his collection *Form as Civilisation*. And it is perhaps just the other side of the coin from 'ornament is crime'. Both allude to the idea that successful forms emerge from good design work. Neither motto is a shorthand (anti-)style guide.

Chapter 5

1 This band of interest also includes non-domestic interiors for, for example, schools, hospitals, and leisure and arts facilities: they are excluded from my analysis here.

2 Charles Eastlake, *Hints on Household Taste* (New York: Dover, 2003), xxi.

3 Ibid., xxiii.

4 Ibid., xxii.

5 Ibid., xxiii.

6 Pevsner quoted in Naylor, 'Morris as a Pioneer', 83.

7 Typically, for example, from *Vogue's* 'Interiors Special', January 2021: 'blur the lines between art and living with design-led homeware'.

8 Museum of the Home, 'Welcome to Museum of the Home', accessed 1 August 2022.

9 A history of domestic life predates the industrial age, of course, but I start with households acquiring mass-produced design goods to create a 'lifestyle', for want of a better word. Also, I use 'Aestheticism' to refer to the historical art movement.

10 Christopher Breward, 'Aestheticism in the Marketplace: Lifestyle and Popular Taste', in *The Cult of Beauty: The Victorian Avant-Garde, 1860–1900*, ed. Stephen Calloway (London: V&A, 2011), 192.

11 Ibid., 204.

12 Ibid., 192.
13 Ibid., 204.
14 Museum of the Home, 'Welcome to Museum of the Home', accessed 1 August 2022.
15 Donnelly, *Christopher Dresser*, 30.
16 Ibid., 30, quoted from the company's prospectus.
17 Ibid., 30, also quoted from the company's prospectus.
18 Liberty & Co. opened in 1875; Morris & Co. in 1877. Liberty still trades on the same principles that 'Liberty is a movement; dedicated to discovery animated by arts, culture, design and the pursuit of beauty – committed to bringing good design to all' (quote from Liberty advertising material included with a purchase from the shop, 2021).
19 It has been noted here too in respect of Charlotte Perriand's work getting good design into people's everyday lives at affordable prices.
20 Penny Sparke, 'Furnishing the Aesthetic Interior: Manuals and Theories', in Calloway, *Cult of Beauty*, 124–33.
21 Dominic Bradbury, *The Iconic Interior: 1900 to the Present* (London: Thames & Hudson, 2020), 13.
22 Charlotte Perkins Gilman, *The Home: Its Work and Influence* (London: William Heinemann, 1904), 3.
23 Ibid., 3.
24 Ibid., 4.
25 Ibid., 4.
26 Ibid., 143.
27 Ibid., 143.
28 Ibid., 145.
29 Ibid., 148.
30 Le Corbusier, *Towards a New Architecture.*
31 Ibid., 101.
32 Ibid., 103.
33 Ibid., 114.
34 Ibid., 115.
35 Ibid., 115.
36 For a broadly cultural and sociological view of modernism and domestic interiors, see, for example, Penny Sparke's *The Modern Interior*

(London: Reaktion Books, 2008). She argues that modernist designers mobilized design ideas about utility and efficiency in mass production to introduce equivalent social and political aims into private lives. I would argue that while the mass design of domestic interiors might well have placed modernist designers and their values in pole position to determine aspects of private, everyday lives, still the aesthetic quality of everyday lives was ultimately at stake and assessable in its terms.

37 Anthony Bertram, *The House: A Machine for Living In* (London: A&C Black, 1935), 5.

38 Ibid., 5.

39 Ibid., 6.

40 Ibid., 1.

41 Ibid., 1.

42 Ibid., 2.

43 Bertram surveys pre-modern forms in everyday use from early Gothic to Art Nouveau, arguing they have served the design aims of their day, before the final two words of *The House: A Machine for Living In*, which are, inviting a modernist aesthetic, 'And now . . .' (ibid., 113).

44 Tim Benton, *The Modernist Home* (London: V&A, 2006), 70.

45 Ibid., 77.

46 Ibid., 77.

47 Frank Pick, 'Maxims for Furnishing', in *Ideal Home Exhibition Catalogue and Review* (London: Daily Mail, 1939), 96.

48 Ibid., 96.

49 Ibid., 96.

50 Ibid., 96.

51 Ibid., 97.

52 Ibid., 97. Interestingly Le Corbusier saw the same problem but failing to see it would apply to his plan for the home too: 'the existing plan of the dwelling-house takes no account of man and is conceived as a furniture store. This scheme of things, favourable enough to the trade of Tottenham Court Road, is of ill omen for society.' London's Tottenham Court Road was at the time a well-known street for fashionable furniture retailers. Le Corbusier, *Towards a New Architecture*, 114.

53 Pick, 'Maxims for Furnishing', 97.

54 Ibid., 97.
55 'Space.Theory Kitchen', advert for spacetheory.com, *Dwell*, May/June 2021, 8.
56 Hamish Bowles, 'Editor's Letter', *The World of Interiors*, June 2022, 15.
57 Mitchell Owens, 'Soap Opera', *The World of Interiors*, May 2022, 52.
58 Liam Freeman, 'Shades of Meaning', *The World of Interiors*, May 2022, 175.
59 Mitchell Owens, 'Ego Tripper', *The World of Interiors*, June 2022, 64.
60 Ibid., 64.
61 Charlotte Fiell and Peter Fiell, *Scandinavian Design* (Koln: Taschen, 2015).
62 I leave examining some aspects of the fourth idea about Scandinavian design's utopian aspirations to Chapter 6, since they largely relate to the general idea of designing utopia, mass housing, and city planning issues which I engage there.
63 Fiell and Fiell, *Scandinavian Design,* 8.
64 Ibid., 10.
65 Ibid., 13.
66 Ibid., 14.
67 Ibid., 14.
68 Bradbury, *Iconic Interior*, 118
69 Ibid., 118.
70 That idea – of the pleasures of using well-made things in convivial settings – is surely already part of the design apology. And in that, the general idea owes as much to Japanese as Scandinavian philosophic underpinnings about experiential, aesthetic value. I have noted that in the contributions of Soetsu Yanagi and Kenya Hara to the design apology. So, having suggested the concept of *hygge* is a Scandinavian 'variation on a theme' of the aesthetic experiences associated with products and places, it might also be added that the Japanese tea ceremony offers another example of cultural variation on a general idea of functional pleasures.
71 Bradbury, *Iconic Interior*, 154.
72 Ibid., 154.
73 Elizabeth A. T. Smith, *Case Study Houses: The Complete CSH Program, 1945–1966* (Koln: Taschen GmbH, 2021), 126.

74 Lawrence Alloway, 'Eames' World', *Architectural Association Journal* 62, no. 804 (1956): 54–55, 54.
75 Fiell and Fiell, Scandinavian Design, 8.
76 Ibid., 18.
77 Quoted in Tom Wilson, *The Story of the Design Museum* (London: Phaidon, 2016), 17.
78 Deyan Sudjic, *Terence Conran: Making Modern Britain* (London: Design Museum), 145.
79 Ibid., 172.
80 Wilson, *Story of the Design Museum*, 17.
81 MacCarthy, *Walter Gropius*, 484.
82 Steierhoffer, McGuirk, and Design Museum, *Home Futures*, 199.
83 Ibid., 199.
84 Ibid., 199.
85 Ibid., 199.
86 Falk, 'Sponsor's Foreword', 5.
87 e-flux Architecture, 'The Diffuse House', January 2021. Thinking about designing homes in the context of new technologies was evident in the 1970s with the Joe Columbo home (see Bradbury, *Iconic Interior*, 20), an early example of the programmable home with a computer at its heart.
88 Joan Ockman, 'The Poetics of Space by Gaston Bachelard', *Harvard Design Magazine* 6 (Fall 1998), no pagination.
89 Gaston Bachelard, *The Poetics of Space*, trans. Maria Jolas (New York: Penguin Books, 2014), 65.
90 Ince, *World of Charles and Ray Eames*, unattributed introductory text for section titled 'At Home with the Eameses', 62.

Chapter 6

1 Hansard, *New Towns Bill*, Volume 422, Section 1091, 8 May 1946.
2 Ebenezer Howard, *Garden Cities of To-Morrow* (London: Faber & Faber, 1946), 150.
3 Lewis Mumford, 'Introduction,' in *Garden Cities of To-Morrow*, ed. Ebenezer Howard (London: Faber & Faber, 1946), 40.

4 Michael Coates, Graeme Brooker, and Sally Stone, *The Visual Dictionary of Interior Architecture and Design* (Lausanne: AVA Publishing SA, 2009), 251.
5 John Boughton, *Municipal Dreams: The Rise and Fall of Council Housing* (London: Verso, 2019), 330.
6 Bertram, *Design*.
7 A US newspaper, similarly, headlined the demolition 'The Death of the City of the Future'. Both views are badly misplaced, part of the 'myth' of Pruitt-Igoe as exemplifying failed *design*. A rounded, contextualized view of the estate's history, including all the socio-economic and demographic factors involved, is given in the film *The Pruitt-Igoe Myth* (Dir. Chad Freidrichs, First Run Features, 2011). In short, it reveals the myth that the failure was one simply of bad, modernist, public housing design. But it also, by that measure, shows the limits of design for changing lives.
8 Le Corbusier, *Towards a New Architecture*, 119. See Chapter 5 for his statement of the problem of the house.
9 Bertram, *Design*, 31.
10 Ibid., 31.
11 Hansard, *New Towns Bill*.
12 'How to live?' was a question on a poster advertising a Werkbund Estate in Germany in the 1920s, for example. The question – and that the answer was/is a radically new way of living – was thematic in modernist housing and urban planning. Its influence is pervasive beyond modernism even if solutions differ.
13 Rosemary Wakeman, *Practicing Utopia: An Intellectual History of the New Town Movement* (Chicago: University of Chicago Press, 2016), 1.
14 Ibid., 1.
15 Ibid., 1.
16 Ibid., 1.
17 Vitruvius Pollio, *Ten Books on Architecture*, trans. Morris Hicky Morgan (Digireads.com, 2009), 15.
18 Ibid., 15.
19 Ibid., 16.
20 Thomas More, *Utopia* (New Haven, CT: Yale University Press, 2001), 57.

21 Ibid., 57.
22 Ibid., 58.
23 Ibid., 58.
24 Parts of London and Paris designed by John Nash and Georges-Eugene Haussmann, respectively, are among notable exceptions that proved the rule of city development is led by the needs of industry for factories and housing for the industrial working-class.
25 Howard, *Garden Cities*, 44.
26 Ibid., 44.
27 Ibid., 49.
28 Ibid., 151.
29 Ibid., 146.
30 In passing I note that Diane Ghirardo has rightly contrasted the 'new communities' of New Deal America and Fascist Italy, despite the fact they shared initial, similar visions about designing communities around land ownership and the supposed 'spiritual benefits' accrued by it. Howard's garden cities ideal linked 'the land' with 'better, happier people', but his notion of 'land' is essentially natural and aesthetic, and his design goals are primarily about our personal well-being rather than some disciplined, social order.
31 Kathleen James-Chakraborty, 'Between Revolution and Reform', in *Bauhaus: Art as Life*, ed. Juliette Desorgues, Corinna Gardner, Leila Hasham, Catherine Ince, and Lydia Yee (London: Barbican Art Gallery, 2012), 18.
32 Walter Gropius, *Programme of the Staaliche Bauhaus in Weimar,* 1919. Reprinted in Desorgues et al., *Bauhaus*, 15.
33 Ibid., 15.
34 Desorgues et al., *Bauhaus*. See catalogue text, 219.
35 Sudjic, *B Is for Bauhaus*, 83.
36 Loos, 'Ornament and Education', in Mitchell, *Ornament and Crime*, 189.
37 Ibid., 189.
38 Kate Arnaud, 'A Paper Paradise', in *Utopia: The Avant-Garde, Modernism and (Im)possible Life*, ed. David Ayers, Benedikt Hjartarson, Tomi Huttunen, and Harri Veivo (Berlin: De Gruyter, 2015), 271. The title alludes to the fact that the architectural plans never got beyond

drawings and words; and perhaps were never intended to but were essentially 'concept' buildings and cities or, in other words, 'utopias'.

39 Ibid., 272.

40 Chapter headings from Jane Alison, Marie-Ange Brayer, Frederic Migayrou, and Neil Spiller, eds., *Future City: Experiment and Utopia in Architecture, 1956–2006* (London: Barbican Art Gallery, 2006).

41 Alison et al., *Future City*, 37.

42 Ibid., 37.

43 Henri Lefebvre, *Toward an Architecture of Enjoyment* (Minnesota: University of Minnesota Press, 2014).

44 Ibid., 16.

45 Ibid., 5.

46 Ibid., 152.

47 Ibid., 152.

48 Ibid.; see also Lukasz Stanek, 'Introduction,' in *Toward an Architecture of Enjoyment*, ed. Henri Lefebvre (Minnesota: University of Minnesota Press, 2014), xviii.

49 Jadwiga Urbanik, ed., *A Way to Modernity: The Werkbund Estates, 1927–1932* (Wroclaw: Museum of Architecture in Wroclaw, 2016), 18.

50 The Weissenhof Model Werkbund Housing Estate in Stuttgart, 1927, detailed in Urbanik, *Way to Modernity*, 32–83.

51 Quoted in Urbanik, *Way to Modernity*, 45.

52 Read, *Art and Industry*, 32. The housing estate's architects included Gropius. Read stated in *Poetry and Anarchism* (London: Faber & Faber, 1938) that Lin Yutang's *The Importance of Living* – with its chapters on the importance of loafing, the sensuousness of human happiness, and the like – expressed 'the outlook on life with which I most sympathize', 121.

53 Read, *Art and Industry*, 32.

54 Ibid., 30.

55 Ibid., 39.

56 Think of the role of so-called 'starchitects' in major urban design projects in the late twentieth and early twenty-first centuries.

57 David Garrard, *Modern Housing of East London* (London: Open City, n.d.). Tour guide map and text; unpaginated.

58 Lewis Mumford, *The Highway and the City* (London: Secker & Warburg, 1964), 33.

59 Ibid., 30.
60 Ibid., 33.
61 Ibid., 33.
62 Jean-Louis Cohen, *Le Corbusier* (Bonn: Taschen, 2004), 58.
63 Ibid., 57.
64 For the politics and planning of Chandigarh in the 1950s, see Maristella Casciato, 'A New Town Planned Literally from A to Z', in *Chandigarh 1956: Photographs by Ernst Scheidegger*, ed. Stanislaus von Moos (Zurich: Scheidegger and Spiess, 2010), 21–44. For that background and Chandigarh's development into the twenty-first century, see also Vinayak Bharne, 'Le Corbusier's Ruin: The Changing Face of Chandigarh's Capitol', *Journal of Architectural Education* 64, no. 2 (March 2011): 99–112.
65 Casciato, 'New Town', 27.
66 Nehru quoted in Stanislaus von Moos, 'Chandigarh 1956', in von Moos, *Chandigarh 1956*, 17.
67 Le Corbusier quoted in Vittorio Franchetti Pardo, *Le Corbusier* (London: Thames & Hudson, 1971), 30.
68 My main source for the general early history of the planning and building of Chandigarh is von Moos, *Chandigarh 1956*.
69 Bharne, 'Le Corbusier's Ruin', 99.
70 Casciato, 'New Town', 27. Casciato also provides an account of the complex interpersonal and professional relationships that played out at Chandigarh, between Le Corbusier, Drew and Maxwell Fry, and with Indian architects and officials. While no doubt generalizable to all major urban design projects, these concerns can be set aside here, given my focus on the lived experience of Chandigarh.
71 Sharon Irish, 'Intimacy and Monumentality in Chandigarh, North India: Le Corbusier's Capitol Complex and Nek Chand Saini's Rock Garden', *Journal of Aesthetic Education* 38, no. 2 (Summer 2004): 105–15.
72 Irish, 'Intimacy and Monumentality', 105.
73 Ibid.
74 Ibid.
75 Ibid.
76 Ibid., 112.
77 Ibid., 113.

78 So, perhaps part of the function of some government buildings is to be 'monumental', to be awe-inspiring, and to present large spaces signifying mass public engagement (which impact political processes).
79 William J. R. Curtis, 'Le Corbusier: The Life of Forms', *The Architectural Review* 224, no. 1340 (October 2008): 84–87; 85.
80 Le Corbusier, *Aircraft* (London: The Studio Ltd, 1935).
81 Ibid., Section 9, Photograph 96 (Note that the book is not paginated beyond the frontispiece; further text appears alongside numbered photographs).
82 Ibid., 13.
83 Ibid., Section 10 heading.
84 Ibid., 11.
85 Ibid., Section 12, Photograph 108.
86 Ibid., Section 13, Photograph 123.
87 See Graham Greene, *The Third Man* (London: Vintage, 2019), 86.
88 This is argued by Frederick Etchells, in his introduction to Le Corbusier's *The City of To-morrow and Its Planning* (New York: Dover, 1987), when he notes the basic functional requirements of city life identified by Le Corbusier, like decent housing, good transport within the city, light and air for out-of-door exercise and recreation, plus sanitation, and energy and water supply. In *Aircraft* too, Le Corbusier is concerned that cities should properly (and were failing) to provide 'pleasures of living: decent dwellings . . . cities which perform their function, cities calm and purposeful' (Section 10, Photograph 101).
89 Bharne, 'Le Corbusier's Ruin', 110.
90 Ibid., 111. A hope dashed, perhaps, by Chandigarh's award of World Heritage status in 2016.
91 Rupal Rathore, 'The Making and Razing of Mumbai's Chawls', *Disegno: The Quarterly Journal of Design* 32 (Spring 2022): 104–16, 116.
92 Oorvi Sharma, 'Inverted Grounds; Tethered Geographies', *Disegno: The Quarterly Journal of Design* 31 (Winter 2021/22): 42–59, 43.
93 Sharma, 'Inverted Grounds', 47.
94 See them photographed in their sci-fi 'House of the Future' at the 1956 Ideal Home Exhibition, London, in Alison et al., *Future City*, 58.
95 Boughton, *Municipal Dreams*.

96 Ibid., 139.

97 Ibid., 141.

98 Ibid., 142.

99 Ibid., 143.

100 Hampstead Garden Suburb Design Study Group, *Hampstead Garden Suburb: The Care and Appreciation of Its Architectural Heritage* (London: HGS Design Study Group, 1977), 12.

101 Ibid., 12.

102 Ibid., 9.

103 Ibid., 9.

104 Ibid., 9.

105 Elizabeth A. T. Smith, 'Icons of Mid-Century Modernism: The Case Study Houses', in Smith, *Case Study Houses*, 9.

106 Ibid., 33.

107 Ibid., 33.

108 Maurice Cox and Rahul Mehrotra, 'A Civil Society', *Harvard Design Magazine* 48 (2021): 83.

109 Marc Norman, 'The New Social Housing', *Harvard Design Magazine* 48 (2021): 124–26.

110 *Harvard Design Magazine* 48 (2021).

111 The possible sources, too, in early twentieth-century science fiction of Sant'Elia's work is noted in Esther Da Costa Meyer, *The Work of Antonio Sant'Elia: Retreat into the Future* (New Haven, CT: Yale University Press, 1995), 137.

112 Antonio Sant'Elia, 'Manifesto of Futurist Architecture', in *Futurist Manifestos*, ed. Umbro Apollonio (Boston: MFA Publications, 1970), 160–72, 171.

113 Ibid., 160.

114 Ibid., 160 and 169.

115 Elizabeth Denby, *Europe Re-housed* (London: George Allen & Unwin, 1938), 256.

116 Ibid., 273.

117 Ibid., 273.

118 Ibid., 274.

119 Ibid., 275.

120 Bertram, *Design*, 21.

121 See Oliver Green, *Frank Pick's London: Art, Design and the Modern City* (London: V&A, 2013). I have noted Pick's ideas on design in relation to furnishing: in passing then, his range of design interests, from chairs to city planning, again witnesses the extent of the design apology's interests and goals.

122 Ibid., 15.

123 Ralph Tubbs, *Living in Cities* (Harmondsworth: Penguin Books, 1942).

124 Ibid., 29.

125 See US Department of Energy, 'Solar Decathlon', accessed August 2022.

126 Charles Montgomery, *The Happy City: Transforming Our Loves through Urban Design* (London: Penguin Books, 2015).

127 Ibid., 15.

128 Ibid., 42. Montgomery notes too that designers have long promised to nurture the mind and soul of society: he gives the example of the 'City Beautiful' movement in America at the turn of the twentieth century and Daniel Burnham's model city, a new Chicago, 'scoured clean of any signs of poverty' (ibid., 23). It was a similarly austere plan by Edward Bellamy, in his utopian novel *Looking Backward*, in the United States in the 1880s that prompted William Morris's counter-utopia.

129 Montgomery, *Happy City*, 42.

130 Nairn, *Outrage*, 451.

131 Ibid., 451.

132 Ibid., 451.

133 These are needs he lists; others may be added though without altering the general means-end argument.

134 Nairn, *Outrage*, 452.

135 See Chapter 3.

Conclusion

1 Rams, 'Foreword', in Kemp, *Dieter Rams*, 7.

2 McGuirk, 'Introduction', in Design Museum, *Waste Age*, 12.

3 'Dwell asks', *Dwell*, September/October 2021, 24.

4 Zara Arshad, 'Whose Future?', *Disegno: The Quarterly Journal of Design* 33 (Summer 2022): 51–62.

5 Ibid., 52.

6 David Pye, *The Nature and Art of Workmanship* (Cambridge: Cambridge University Press, 1968), 71.

7 Karel Capek, *R.U.R. (Rossum's Universal Robots)*, trans. Paul Selver and adapted for the English Stage by Nigel Playfair (London: Oxford University Press, 1923), 67.

8 Ibid., 66.

9 Ibid., 67.

10 Herbert Read, *The Redemption of the Robot: My Encounter with Education through Art* (New York: Trident Press, 1966).

11 Lara Lesmes and Fredrik Hellberg, 'Design for the Real(v) World', *Disegno: The Quarterly Journal of Design* 32 (Spring 2022): 117–28.

12 Rams, 'Foreword,' in Kemp, *Dieter Rams*, 7.

13 Le Corbusier, *Towards a New Architecture*, 102.

14 Nairn, *Outrage*, 455.

15 Harold John Massingham, *Through the Wilderness* (London: Cobden-Sanderson, 1935), 37.

16 Ibid., 9.

17 Ibid., 8.

18 Rex Warner, *The Aerodrome* (London: Penguin Books, 1944), 192.

Bibliography

Alison, Jane, Marie-Ange Brayer, Frederic Migayrou, and Neil Spiller, eds. *Future City: Experiment and Utopia in Architecture, 1956–2006*. London: Barbican Art Gallery, 2006.

Alloway, Lawrence. 'Eames' World'. *Architectural Association Journal* 62, no. 804 (1956): 54–55.

Aristotle. *The Nicomachean Ethics*, translated by J. A. K. Thomson. London: Penguin Books, 2004.

Arnaud, Kate. 'A Paper Paradise'. In *Utopia: The Avant-Garde, Modernism and (Im)possible Life*, edited by David Ayers, Benedikt Hjartarson, Tomi Huttunen, and Harri Veivo, 259–74. Berlin: De Gruyter, 2015.

Arshad, Zara. 'Whose Future?' *Disegno: The Quarterly Journal of Design* 33 (Summer 2022): 51–62.

Ayers, David, Benedikt Hjartarson, Tomi Huttunen, and Harri Veivo, eds. *Utopia: The Avant-Garde, Modernism and (Im)possible Life*. Berlin: De Gruyter, 2015.

Bachelard, Gaston. *The Poetics of Space*, translated by Maria Jolas. New York: Penguin Books, 2014.

Bean, Jonathan. 'Review of *Routledge Companion to Design Studies* (2016)'. *Journal of Design History* 30, no. 2 (May 2017): 243–45.

Beardsley, Monroe. *Aesthetics*. Indianapolis, IN: Hackett, 1981.

Beerbohm, Max. *Rossetti and His Circle*. New Haven, CT: Yale University Press, 1987.

Benton, Tim. *The Modernist Home*. London: V&A, 2006.

Bertram, Anthony. *Design*. London: Pelican, 1938.

Bertram, Anthony. *Design in Everyday Things*. London: British Broadcasting Corporation, 1937.

Bertram, Anthony. *The House: A Machine for Living In*. London: A&C Black, 1935.

Bharne, Vinayak. 'Le Corbusier's Ruin: The Changing Face of Chandigarh's Capitol'. *Journal of Architectural Education* 64, no. 2 (March 2011): 99–112.

Boos, Florence. *Socialist Aesthetics & the Shadows of Amiens*. London: William Morris Society, 2011.

Borgmann, Albert. 'The Depth of Design'. In *Design Philosophy Reader*, edited by Anne-Marie Willis, 22–25. London: Bloomsbury, 2019.

Boughton, John. *Municipal Dreams: The Rise and Fall of Council Housing*. London: Version, 2019.

Bowles, Hamish. 'Editor's Letter', *The World of Interiors*, 15 June 2022.

Bradbury, Dominic. *The Iconic Interior: 1900 to the Present*. London: Thames & Hudson, 2020.

Bradley, Darren. 'Yesterday's Vision of Tomorrow'. *The Modernist* 33 (December 2019): 12–13.

Breward, Christopher. 'Aestheticism in the Marketplace: Lifestyle and Popular Taste'. In *The Cult of Beauty: The Victorian Avant-Garde, 1860–1900*, edited by Stephen Calloway, 192–205. London: V&A, 2011.

Buchanan, Richard, and Victor Margolin, eds. *Discovering Design: Explorations in Design Studies*. Chicago: University of Chicago Press, 1995.

Capek, Karel. 'An Invention'. In *Believe in People: The Essential Karel Capek*, translated with an introduction by Sarka Tobrmanova-Kuhnova, 142–44. London: Faber & Faber.

Capek, Karel. *R.U.R. (Rossum's Universal Robots)*, translated by Paul Selver and adapted for the English stage by Nigel Playfair. London: Oxford University Press, 1923.

Casciato, Maristella. 'A New Town Planned Literally from A to Z'. In *Chandigarh 1956: Photographs by Ernst Scheidegger*, edited by Stanislaus von Moos, 21–44. Zurich: Scheidegger and Spiess, 2010.

Coates, Michael, Graeme Brooker, and Sally Stone. *The Visual Dictionary of Interior Architecture and Design*. Lausanne: AVA Publishing SA, 2009.

Cohen, Jean-Louis. *Le Corbusier*. Bonn: Taschen, 2004.

Cox, Maurice, and Rahul Mehrotra. 'A Civil Society'. *Harvard Design Magazine* 48 (2021): 82–85.

Curtis, William J. R. 'Le Corbusier: The Life of Forms'. *The Architectural Review* 224, no. 1340 (October 2008): 84–87.

Czerwinski, Michael. *Fifty Chairs That Changed the World*. London: Octopus, 2011.

Davies, David. 'Sibley and the Limits of Everyday Aesthetics'. *Journal of Aesthetic Education* 49, no. 3 (Fall 2015): 50–65.

de Dampierre, Florence. *Chairs: A History*. New York: Harry N. Abrams, 2006.

Demetrios, Eames. 'A Contemporary Practice: The Eameses in the 1940s'. In *The World of Charles and Ray Eames*, edited by Catherine Ince, 20–40. London: Thames & Hudson, 2015.

Denby, Elizabeth. *Europe Re-housed*. London: George Allen & Unwin, 1938.

Design Museum. *Designs of the Year*. London: Design Museum, 2011.

Design Museum. *Designs of the Year*. London: Design Museum, 2013.

Design Museum. *Designs of the Year*. London: Design Museum, 2017.

Design Museum. *Designs of the Year*. London: Design Museum, 2019.

Design Museum. *Designs of the Year*. London: Design Museum, 2020.

Desorgues, Juliette, Corinna Gardner, Leila Hasham, Catherine Ince, and Lydia Yee. *Bauhaus: Art as Life*. London: Koenig Books, 2012.

Dewey, John. *Art as Experience*. New York: Minton, Balch & Company, 1934.

Donnelly, Max. *Christopher Dresser: Design Pioneer*. London: Thames & Hudson, 2021.

Dorst, Kees. 'But Is It Art?' In *Design and Art*, edited by Alex Coles, 10–18. London: Whitechapel Gallery, 2007.

Dowling, Christopher. 'The Aesthetics of Daily Life'. *British Journal of Aesthetics* 50, no. 3 (2010): 225–42.

Drexler, Arthur. *Charles Eames: Furniture from the Design Collection, the Museum of Modern Art, New York*. New York: The Museum of Modern Art, 1973.

Dreyfuss, Henry. *Designing for People*. New York: Simon and Schuster, 1955.

Eastlake, Charles. *Hints on Household Taste*. New York: Dover, [1878] 2003.

Elliott, Mark, and Nicholas Thomas, eds. *Gifts and Discoveries*. London: Scala, 2011.

Englund, Magnus. 'Bend It like Morrison'. *Disegno: The Quarterly Journal of Design* 30 (2021): 78–83.

Fiell, Charlotte, and Peter Fiell. *Scandinavian Design*. Koln: Taschen, 2015.

Fiell, Charlotte, and Peter Fiell. *The Story of Design*. London: Goodman Fiell, 2013.

Foot, Philippa. *Natural Goodness*. Oxford: Clarendon Press, 2001.

Forsey, Jane. *The Aesthetics of Design*. Oxford: Oxford University Press, 2013.

Freeman, Liam. 'Shades of Meaning', *The World of Interiors*, May 2022, 166–83.

Garrahan, Rachel. 'The Watch That Saved Cartier', *Vogue*, May 2021, 118–19.

Garrard, David. *Modern Housing of East London*. London: Open City, n.d.

Ghirardo, Diane. *Building New Communities: New Deal America and Fascist Italy*. Princeton, NJ: Princeton University Press, 1989.

Giacomelli, Francesca. 'Enzo Mari Was a Universe'. *Disegno: The Quarterly Journal of Design* 28 (Spring 2021): 123–36.

Gilman, Charlotte Perkins. *The Home: Its Work and Influence*. London: William Heinemann, 1904.

Glickfield, Elizabeth. 'Futureheads'. *Design Reviewed* 1 (January 2023): 44–51.

Green, Oliver. *Frank Pick's London: Art, Design and the Modern City*. London: V&A, 2013.

Greene, Graham. *The Third Man*. London: Vintage, 2019.

Gropius, Walter. *Programme of the Staaliche Bauhaus in Weimar*, 1919. Reprinted in *Bauhaus: Art as Life*, edited by Juliette Desorgues, Corinna Gardner, Leila Hasham, Catherine Ince, and Lydia Yee, 14–17. London: Koenig Books, 2012.

Guyer, Paul. 'History of Modern Aesthetics'. In *The Oxford Handbook of Aesthetics*, edited by Jerrold Levinson, 25–62. Oxford: Oxford University Press, 2003.

Hamilton, Andy. 'The Aesthetics of Design'. In *Fashion and Philosophy*, edited by Jeanette Kennett and Jessica Wolfendale, 51–69. London: Blackwell, 2011.

Hamilton, Andy. 'The Anatomy of Architecture'. In *Scruton's Aesthetics*, edited by Andy Hamilton and Nick Zangwill, 177–212. London: Palgrave Macmillan, 2012.

Hamilton, Andy, and Nick Zangwill, eds. *Scruton's Aesthetics*. London: Palgrave Macmillan, 2012.

Hampstead Garden Suburb Design Study Group. *Hampstead Garden Suburb: The Care and Appreciation of Its Architectural Heritage*. London: HGS Design Study Group, 1977.

Hansard. *New Towns Bill*, Volume 422, Section 1091, 8 May 1946.

Hara, Kenya. *Designing Japan: A Future Built on Aesthetics*, translated by Maggie Kinser and Yukiko Naito. Zurich: Lars Muller, 2018.

Hatherley, Owen. 'Back to the Red House: William Morris after Reform and Revolution'. In *How I Became a Socialist*, edited by William Morris, 1–15. London: Verso, 2020.

Hodge, Susie. *What Makes Great Design: 80 Masterpieces Explained*. London: Francis Lincoln, 2014.

Howard, Ebenezer. *Garden Cities of To-Morrow*, edited with a preface by F. J. Osborn. London: Faber & Faber, [1898] 1946.

Huppatz, D. J. *Design: The Key Concepts*. London: Bloomsbury Visual Arts, 2019.

Ince, Catherine, ed. *The World of Charles and Ray Eames*. London: Thames & Hudson, 2015.

Irish, Sharon. 'Intimacy and Monumentality in Chandigarh, North India: Le Corbusier's Capitol Complex and Nek Chand Saini's Rock Garden'. *Journal of Aesthetic Education* 38, no. 2 (Summer 2004): 105–15.

Irvin, Sherri. 'Is Aesthetic Experience Possible?' In *Aesthetics and the Sciences of Mind*, edited by Greg Currie, Matthew Kieran, Aaron Meskin, and Jon Robson, 37–56. Oxford: Oxford University Press, 2014.

Irvin, Sherri. 'The Pervasiveness of the Aesthetic in Ordinary Experience'. *British Journal of Aesthetics* 48, no. 1 (2008): 29–44.

James-Chakraborty, Kathleen. 'Between Revolution and Reform'. In *Bauhaus: Art as Life*, edited by Juliette Desorgues, Corinna Gardner, Leila Hasham, Catherine Ince, and Lydia Yee, 18–20. London: Koenig Books, 2012.

Jones, Barbara. *The Unsophisticated Arts*. London: The Architectural Press, 1951.

Kapos, Peter. 'Counterpoints'. *Disegno: The Quarterly Journal of Design* 30 (Autumn 2021): 53–59.

Kemp, Klaus, ed. *Dieter Rams: The Complete Works*. London: Phaidon, 2020.

Kirkham, Pat. *History of Design*. New Haven, CT: Yale University Press, 2013.

Kropotkin, Peter. *The Conquest of Bread*. London: Penguin Books, [1892] 2015.

Kvetkova, Zuzana. 'Asking the Right Questions', interview with Christian Madsbjerg by Zuzana Kvetkova, *Backstage Talks: Dialogues on Design and Business* 5, 2020.

Kvetkova, Zuzana. 'Editorial', *Backstage Talks: Dialogues on Design and Business* 5, 2020.

Leach, Bernard. *A Potter in Japan: 1952–1954*. London: Unicorn, 2015.

Le Corbusier. *Aircraft*. London: The Studio, 1935.

Le Corbusier. *The City of To-morrow and Its Planning*, translated with an introduction by Frederick Etchells. New York: Dover, 1987.

Le Corbusier. *Towards a New Architecture*, translated from the French by Frederick Etchells. London: The Architectural Press, 1946.

Lefebvre, Henri. *Toward an Architecture of Enjoyment*. Minnesota: University of Minnesota Press, 2014.

Lesmes, Lara, and Fredrik Hellberg. 'Design for the Real(v) World'. *Disegno: The Quarterly Journal of Design* 32 (2022): 117–28.

Lethaby, William. 'Education for Appreciation or for Production?' In *Form in Civilization*, edited by William Lethaby, 133–38. Oxford: Oxford University Press, 1922.

Lethaby, William. 'Education of the Architect'. In *Form in Civilization*, edited by William Lethaby, 122–32. Oxford: Oxford University Press, [1917] 1922.

Loewy, Raymond. *Industrial Design*. London: Fourth Estate, 1988.

Loewy, Raymond. *Never Leave Well Enough Alone*. New York: Simon and Schuster, 1951.

London Metropolitan University. *The Frederick Parker Collection: A Selection of Chairs*. London: London Metropolitan University, n.d.

Loos, Adolf. 'Chairs'. In *Ornament and Crime: Thoughts on Design and Materials*, translated by Shaun Whiteside, 163–72. London: Penguin, 2019.

Loos, Adolf. 'Glass and China'. In *Ornament and Crime: Thoughts on Design and Materials*, translated by Shaun Whiteside, 173–84. London: Penguin, 2019.

Loos, Adolf. 'Ornament and Education'. In *Ornament and Crime: Selected Essays*, translated by Michael Mitchell, 184–89. Riverside, CA: Ariadne Press, 1998.

MacCarthy, Fiona. *Walter Gropius*. London: Faber & Faber, 2020.

MacGregor, Neil. *The History of the World in 100 Objects*. London: Allen Lane, 2010.

Massingham, Harold John. *Through the Wilderness*. London: Cobden-Sanderson, 1935.

McCracken, Janet. 'Book Reviews'. *Journal of Aesthetics and Art Criticism* 58, no. 1 (2000): 76–79.

McCracken, Janet. 'Why We Love Our Phones: A Case Study in the Aesthetics of Gadgets'. In *Comparative Everyday Aesthetics*, edited by Eva Kit Wah Man and Jeffrey Petts, 201–20. Amsterdam: Amsterdam University Press, 2023.

McGuirk, Justin. 'Introduction'. In *Charlotte Perriand: The Modern Life*, edited by Design Museum, 7–14. London: Design Museum, 2021.

McGuirk, Justin. 'Introduction'. In *Waste Age*, edited by Design Museum, 7–15. London: Design Museum, 2021.

McLeod, Mary. 'Charlotte Perriand's *Art de Vivre*'. In *Charlotte Perriand: An Art of Living*, edited by Mary McLeod, 10–21. New York: Harry N. Abrams, 2003.

Melchionne, Kevin. 'Aesthetic Experience in Everyday Life: A Reply to Dowling'. *British Journal of Aesthetics* 51, no. 4 (2011): 437–42.

Meyer, Esther Da Costa. *The Work of Antonio Sant'Elia: Retreat into the Future*. New Haven, CT: Yale University Press, 1995.

Moers, Ellen. *The Dandy*. London: Secker & Warburg, 1960.

Montgomery, Charles. *The Happy City: Transforming Our Lives through Urban Design*. London: Penguin Books, 2015.

More, Thomas. *Utopia*. New Haven, CT: Yale University Press, [1516] 2001.

Morris, William. 'A Factory as It Might Be'. In *William Morris: Selected Writings*, edited by George Douglas Howard Cole, 646–54. London: Nonesuch Press, 1934.

Morris, William. 'How I Became a Socialist'. In *William Morris: Selected Writings*, edited by George Douglas Howard Cole, 655–59. London: Nonesuch Press, 1934.

Mumford, Lewis. *The Highway and the City*. London: Secker & Warburg, 1964.

Mumford, Lewis. 'Introduction'. In *Ebenezer Howard: Garden Cities of To-Morrow*, edited by Ebenezer Howard, 41–49. London: Faber & Faber, 1946.

Munari, Bruno. *Design as Art*, translated by Patrick Creagh. London: Penguin, 2008.

Myerson, Jeremy. 'Sometimes Frivolous, Sometimes Philosophical'. *Disegno: The Quarterly Journal of Design* 29 (Summer 2021): 18–23.

Nairn, Ian. *Nairn's London*. London: Penguin Books, [1966] 2014.

Nairn, Ian. *Outrage*. London: The Architectural Press, 1956.

Nairn, Ian, and Nikolaus Pevsner. *Sussex: West (Pevsner Architectural Guides: The Buildings of England)*. New Haven, CT: Yale University Press, [1965] 2019.

Naylor, Gillian. 'Morris as a Pioneer of Modern Design'. In *William Morris Now*, edited by Roger Simon, 81–86. London: Institute of Contemporary Arts, 1984.

Norman, Marc. 'The New Social Housing'. *Harvard Design Magazine* 48 (2021): 124–26.

Objectified. [Film]. Dir. Gary Hustwit, Submarine Deluxe, Streaming Video, 2009.

Ockman, Joan. 'The Poetics of Space by Gaston Bachelard'. *Harvard Design Magazine* 6 (Fall 1998), unpaginated online.

Opara, Eddie. 'Design Is about Creating Systems, not Solving Problems', *Backstage Talks: Dialogues on Design and Business* 5, 2020.

Owens, Mitchell. 'Ego Trippers', *The World of Interiors*, June 2022, 63–64.

Owens, Mitchell. 'Soap Opera', *The World of Interiors*, May 2022, 52–54.

Packard, Vance. *The Waste Makers*. London: Longmans, 1961.

Pardo, Vittorio Franchetti. *Le Corbusier*. London: Thames & Hudson, 1971.

Parsons, Glenn. *The Philosophy of Design*. Cambridge: Polity Press, 2016.

Perriand, Charlotte. 'Ambience'. In *Charlotte Perriand: An Art of Living*, edited by Mary McLeod, 262–63. New York: Harry N. Abrams, 2003.

Perriand, Charlotte. 'The Art of Dwelling'. In *Charlotte Perriand: An Art of Living*, edited by Mary McLeod, 262. New York: Harry N. Abrams, 2003.

Perriand, Charlotte. 'The Family Dwelling: Its Economic and Social Development'. In *Charlotte Perriand: An Art of Living*, edited by Mary McLeod, 255–56. New York: Harry N. Abrams, 2003.

Perriand, Charlotte. 'Wood or Metal?' In *Charlotte Perriand: An Art of Living*, edited by Mary McLeod, 251–53. New York: Harry N. Abrams, 2003.

Petts, Jeffrey. 'Aesthetic Experience and the Revelation of Value'. *Journal of Aesthetics and Art Criticism* 58, no. 1 (2000): 61–71.

Pevsner, Nikolaus. *Pioneers of Modern Design: From William Morris to Walter Gropius*. London: Penguin Books, 1991.

Picchi, Francesca. 'A Thing of Beauty Is a Joy Forever'. In *James Irvine*, edited by Picchi, Francesca and Marialaura Rossiello Irvine, 23–31. London: Phaidon, 2015.

Picchi, Francesca, and Marialaura Rossiello Irvine, eds. *James Irvine*. London: Phaidon, 2015.

Pick, Frank. 'Maxims for Furnishing'. In *Ideal Home Exhibition Catalogue and Review*, edited by Frank Pick, 96–97. London: Daily Mail, 1939.

Plato. 'Republic'. In *The Collected Dialogues*, edited by Edith Hamilton and Huntingdon Cairns, 575–844. Princeton, NJ: University Press, 1994.

Pollock, Naomi. *Japanese Design: A Complete Sourcebook*. London: Thames & Hudson, 2020.

Potter, Norman. 'Is a Designer an Artist?' In *Design and Art*, edited by Alex Coles, 29–33. London: Whitechapel Gallery, 2007.

Pruitt-Igoe Myth. [Film]. Dir. Chad Freidrichs, First Run Features, 2011.

Pye, David. *The Nature and Art of Workmanship*. Cambridge: Cambridge University Press, 1968.

Pye, David. *The Nature of Design*. London: Studio Vista, 1964.

Rams, Dieter. 'Foreword'. In *Dieter Rams: The Complete Works*, edited by Klaus Kemp, 6–7. London: Phaidon, 2020.

Rams. [Film]. Dir. Gary Hustwit, First Film Corp, Streaming Video, 2018.

Rathore, Rupal. 'The Making and Razing of Mumbai's Chawls'. *Disegno: The Quarterly Journal of Design* 32 (Spring 2022): 104–16.

Read, Herbert. *Art and Industry*. London: Faber & Faber, 1934.

Read, Herbert. *Poetry and Anarchism*. London: Faber & Faber, 1938.

Read, Herbert. *The Redemption of the Robot: My Encounter with Education through Art*. New York: A Trident Press Book, 1966.

Reader, Soran. 'Aristotle on Necessities and Needs'. In *The Philosophy of Need*, edited by Soran Reader, 113–35. Cambridge: Cambridge University Press, 2005.

Saito, Yuriko. *Aesthetics of Care: Practice in Everyday Life*. London: Bloomsbury Academic, 2022.

Saito, Yuriko. *Aesthetics of the Familiar: Everyday Life and World-Making*. Oxford: Oxford University Press, 2019.

Saito, Yuriko. *Everyday Aesthetics*. Oxford: Oxford University Press, 2007.

Sandberg Falk, Anna. 'Sponsor's Foreword'. In *Home Futures*, edited by Eszter Steierhoffer, Justin McGuirk, and Design Museum, 5. London: Design Museum, 2018.

Sant'Elia, Antonio. 'Manifesto of Futurist Architecture'. In *Futurist Manifestos*, edited by Umbro Apollonio, 160–72. Boston: MFA Publications, 1970.

Sartwell, Crispin. 'Aesthetics of the Everyday'. In *The Oxford Handbook of Aesthetics*, edited by Jerrold Levinson, 761–70. Oxford: Oxford University Press, 2003.

Scruton, Roger. 'Aesthetic Education and Design'. *Architecture Philosophy* 3, no. 2 (2018): 214–31.

Scruton, Roger. 'A Bit of Help from Wittgenstein'. *British Journal of Aesthetics* 51, no. 3 (2011): 309–19.

Semelak, Milan. 'Stop Making the World a Worse Place', *Backstage Talks: Dialogues on Design and Business* 5, 2020, 140–42.

Semper, Gottfried. *Style in the Technical and Tectonic Arts; or Practical Aesthetics*, translated by Harry Francis Malgrave and Michael Robinson. Los Angeles: Getty Research Institute, [1860] 2004.

Sempill, William Francis Forbes. 'Foreword'. In *Design*, edited by Anthony Bertram, vii–viii. London: Penguin Books, 1938.

Sharma, Oorvi. 'Inverted Grounds; Tethered Geographies'. *Disegno: The Quarterly Journal of Design* 31 (Winter 2021/22): 42–59.

Smith, Elizabeth A. T. 'Icons of Mid-Century Modernism: The Case Study Houses'. In *Case Study Houses: The Complete CSH Program, 1945–1966*, edited by Elizabeth A. T. Smith, 9–13. Koln: Taschen GmbH.

Smith, Elizabeth A. T., ed. *Case Study Houses: The Complete CSH Program, 1945–1966*. Koln: Taschen GmbH.

South Bank Exhibition, Festival of Britain, Guide. London: His Majesty's Stationery Office, 1951.

Sparke, Penny. 'Furnishing the Aesthetic Interior: Manuals and Theories'. In *The Cult of Beauty: The Victorian Avant-Garde, 1860–1900*, edited by Stephen Calloway, 124–33. London: V&A, 2011.

Sparke, Penny. *The Modern Interior*. London: Reaktion Books, 2008.

Stanek, Lukasz. 'Introduction'. In *Toward an Architecture of Enjoyment*, edited by Henri Lefebvre, xi–lxi. Minnesota: University of Minnesota Press, 2014.

Stecker, Robert. 'Aesthetic Experience and Aesthetic Value'. *Philosophy Compass* 1, no. 1 (2006): 1–10.

Steierhoffer, Eszter, Justin McGuirk, and Design Museum, *Home Futures*. London: Design Museum, 2018.

Stratford, Oli. 'Designing the Batman'. *Disegno: The Quarterly Journal of Design* 32 (Spring 2022): 7–8.

Stratford, Oli. 'The Only Thing Left to Design Is the Foot'. *Disegno: The Quarterly Journal of Design* 28 (Spring 2021): 83–100.

Stratford, Oli. 'The Sugar Pot'. *Disegno: The Quarterly Journal of Design* 31 (Winter 2021): 3–4.

Sudjic, Deyan. *B Is for Bauhaus: An A–Z of the Modern World*. London: Penguin Books, 2015.

Sudjic, Deyan. 'Introduction'. In *Fifty Chairs That Changed the World*, edited by Michael Czerwinski, 6. London: Octopus, 2009.

Sudjic, Deyan. *The Language of Things*. London: Penguin Books, 2008.

Sudjic, Deyan. *Terence Conran: Making Modern Britain*. London: Design Museum, 2021.

Sulzer, Peter. *Jean Prouve Complete Works, Volume 1: 1917–1933*. Basel: Birkhauser, 2009.

Taylor, Alfred Edward. *Aristotle*. New York: Dover, 1955.

Tubbs, Ralph. *Living in Cities*. Harmondsworth: Penguin Books, 1942.

Urbanik, Jadwiga, ed. *A Way to Modernity: The Werkbund Estates, 1927–1932*. Wroclaw: Museum of Architecture in Wroclaw, 2016.

Vitruvius Pollio. *Ten Books on Architecture*, translated by Morris Hicky Morgan. Digireads.com, 2019.

von Moos, Stanislaus. 'Chandigarh 1956'. In *Chandigarh 1956: Photographs by Ernst Scheidegger*, edited by Stanislaus von Moos, 15–20. Zurich: Scheidegger and Spiess, 2010.

von Moos, Stanilaus, ed. *Chandigarh 1956: Photographs by Ernst Scheidegger*. Zurich: Scheidegger and Spiess, 2010.

Wakeman, Rosemary. *Practicing Utopia: An Intellectual History of the New Town Movement*. Chicago: University of Chicago Press, 2016.

Warner, Rex. *The Aerodrome*. London: Penguin Books, 1944.

Wiggins, David. 'An Idea We Cannot Do Without'. In *The Philosophy of Need*, edited by Soran Reader, 25–50. Cambridge: Cambridge University Press, 2005.

Wiggins, David. *Needs, Values, Truth*. London: Blackwell, 1991.

Williams, Gareth. *Design: An Essential Introduction*. London: Design Museum, 2015.

Willis, Anne-Marie. 'Introduction'. In *The Design Philosophy Reader*, edited by Anne-Marie Willis, 1–8. London: Bloomsbury, 2019.

Wilson, Tom. *The Story of the Design Museum*. London: Phaidon, 2016.

Winters, Edward. 'Against Neatness, and the Neateners Who Would Neaten Us'. In *Scruton's Aesthetics*, edited by Andy Hamilton and Nick Zangwill, 213–33. London: Palgrave Macmillan, 2012.

Wittgenstein, Ludwig. *Lectures & Conversations on Aesthetics, Psychology and Religious Belief*, edited by Cyril Barrett. Oxford: Blackwell, 1966.

Yanagi, Soetsu. 'The Beauty of Miscellaneous Things'. In *The Beauty of Everyday Things*, edited by Soetsu Yanagi, 27–58. London: Penguin Classics, 2018.

Yanagi, Soetsu. 'The Japan Folk Crafts Museum'. In *The Beauty of Everyday Things*, edited by Soetsu Yanagi, 325–46. London: Penguin Classics, 2018.

Yutang, Lin. *The Importance of Living*. New York: The John Day Company, 1937.

Index

Page numbers: Figures are given in *italics* and notes as [page number]n.